A HISTORY MAKER

Alasdair Gray is a stout, elderly, married Glaswegian who lives by painting and writing things. His other books are *Lanark*, *Unlikely Stories Mostly*, *1982 Janine*, *The Fall of Kelvin Walker*, *Lean Tales* (with James Kelman and Agnes Owens), *Old Negatives* (verse), *McGrotty and Ludmilla*, *Something Leather*, *Why Scots Should Rule Scotland*, *Poor Things*, *Ten Tales Tall and True*. He is now writing *The Anthology of Prefaces*, introductions to English vernacular masterpieces by their authors, chronologically arranged with historical and biographical notes, and will complete it before the 21st century, if he is spared.

A HISTORY MAKER

BY ALASDAIR GRAY

FOR CHRIS BOYCE

PENGUIN BOOKS
LONDON 1995

The book is dedicated to Chris Boyce whose
conversation suggested nearly all the science and
some of the fiction. It is also indebted to
Margaret Mead whose *Coming of Age in Samoa*
suggested the form of a kindlier society than
her critics thought possible; also to Bruce
Charlton for medical advice and Scott Pearson
for scholarly research and proof correction.

Designed by Alasdair Gray
Set in Scotland by Joe Murray of EM-DEE
Productions for Dog and Bone typesetting
Printed in England by Clays Ltd., St. Ives plc.

A Cataloguing In Publication record for this
book is available from the British Library. The
International Standard Book Number is
0 14024 803 X

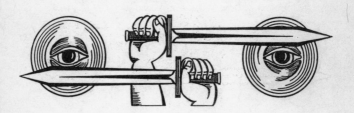

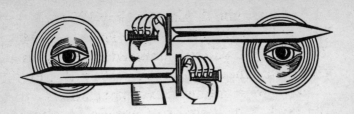

"*Economics*: Old Greek word for the art of keeping a home weatherproof and supplied with what the householders need. For at least three centuries this word was used by British rulers and their advisers to mean *political* housekeeping — the art of keeping their bankers, brokers and rich supporters well supplied with money, often by impoverishing other householders. They used the Greek instead of the English word because it mystified folk who had not been taught at wealthy schools. The rhetoric of plutocratic bosses needed *economics* as the sermons of religious ones needed The Will of God."

— from *The Intelligence Archive of Historical Jargon*.

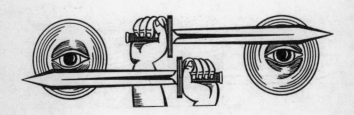

TABLE OF

Map of Saint Mary's Loch, 2220   II

TITLEPAGE and DEDICATION   III

Book Information   IV

EPIGRAPH   V

TABLE of CONTENTS   VI

View of Dryhope Tower, 1820   VIII

Prologue by a Hero's Mother   IX

CONTENTS

CHAPTER One – Public Eye   1

CHAPTER Two – Private Houses   23

CHAPTER Three – Warrior Work   58

CHAPTER Four – Puddock Plot   92

CHAPTER Five – The Henwife   122

Notes Explaining Obscurities   157

Postscript by a Student of Folklore   219

*Dryhope Tower
and Saint Mary's Loch,
Bowerhope to the left on the far shore,
around 1822.*

PROLOGUE

BY A HERO'S MOTHER

BEFORE VANISHING from the open intelligence net Wat Dryhope gave me a printout of the next five chapters saying, "My apology for a botched life, mother. Do what you like with it."

I put it on a shelf behind old encyclopædias. The title scunnered me. Not knowing it was ironical I feared that his memoirs, like those of ancient politicians, would hoist a claim to importance by blaming his failure on wicked enemies and stupid helpers. The words "a botched life" suggested something different but equally dreich: the start of Augustine's Confessions where the saint prepares us for his extraordinary conversion by denouncing his very ordinary early nastiness. I loved Wat most of my gets so *had no wish to read what might make me despise him. Nor could I burn his writing unread. I placed it in easy reach and ignored it for years.*

One grey dank autumn afternoon two months ago I had fed the poultry and was snibbing the henrun gate when I fell down flat and took an hour to regain breath and balance. I have had several tumbles lately, each worse than the last; have also started recalling events of twenty, forty, sixty years ago more clearly than this morning or yesterday. Lying on the cold ground I knew that if not killed by a stroke I must soon join my daughters softening into senile dementia in the house where I was born. On returning to the tower I took Wat's printout from the shelf and dusted it. After filling a glass with uisge beatha I began to read and finished long before nightfall without sipping a drop. Admiration for Wat had become my strongest feeling; also anger with myself for keeping his work so long from the public. Later readings have not lessened my admiration for the clarity of the narration and honesty of the narrator.

A History Maker *tells of seven crucial*

days in the life of a man with all the weaknesses that nearly brought the matriarchy of early modern time to a bad end yet all the strengths that helped it survive, reform, improve. Wat Dryhope, like Julius Caesar describing his Gallic wars, avoids vainglory and self-pity by naming himself in the third person and keeping the tale factual. He also writes so cannily that, like Walter Scott in his best novels, he gives the reader a sense of being at mighty doings. Adroit critics will notice his sly shift from present to past tense in the first chapter. Like Scott he tells a Scottish story in an English easily understood by other parts of the world but leaves the gab of the locals in its native doric. This shows he wanted his story read inside AND outside the Ettrick Forest, and I have warstled to help this by putting among my final notes a glossary of words liable to ramfeezle Sassenachs, North Americans and others with their own variety of English.

Yet with all its art four fifths of Wat's story is proven fact on the testimony of a whole horde of independent witnesses. The first chapter is not only confirmed by public eye records but clearly based on them. These

*records also confirm his account of the
reception before the Ettrick Warrior house,
his platform announcement, his talk with
Archie Crook Cot in the third chapter, and
quotations from public reports and
discussions of the new militarism in the fifth.
Open intelligence archives confirm the
judgement on the Ettrick–Northumberland
cliffside battle by the Council for War
Regulation Sitting in Geneva, and the night
of puddock migrations to fresh water in
southern Scotland that year, and the dates
and wording of the advert and banquet
invitation issued by Cellini's Cloud Circus.*

I have also sent copies of A History Maker
*to everyone I could find who is mentioned
in it. Only Mirren Craig Douglas (that
bitter woman) returned it without comment,
which from her must signify assent. Wat's
brothers Joe and Sandy — his mistresses
Nan and Annie and the Bowerhope twins
— the veterans and servants of the Warrior
house — the sisters who nursed him — I
who schooled him — General Shafto who
took him to the circus — all say he tells the
truth as they recall it. Only the account of
his doings with Meg Mountbenger in the
gruesome fourth chapter are not confirmed*

by another protagonist, and why should he
turn fanciful about her when honest about
others? Some critics say Lawrence's account
of his rape in The Seven Pillars of Wisdom
is an invention by which a lonely masochist
got public sympathy for his queerness.
Perhaps. Nothing else in Lawrence's story
depends on that rape so he may or may not
have tholed it. But after Wat left Bowerhope
that morning only a sore carnal collision
can explain his state when he was found by
the loch side, and explain his remarks to
his sisters, and his story to me, and his
dissemination of a plague which withered
powerplants in every continent but
Antarctica. If still alive Meg is sixty-three.
Should she reappear and deny Wat's story
let none believe her. She was always a
perverse bitch. She was the first of my gets,
but I never liked her.

So I bequeath A History Maker to the
open intelligence, having added to the end
notes explaining what those who ken little
of the past may find bumbazing. For
posterity's sake my notes about the
immediate present are put in the past tense
too, since the present soon will be. Wat was
a scholar and a fighter. His tale of warfare,

*love and skulduggery also meditates on
human change. It antidotes a dangerous
easy-oasy habit of thinking the modern
world at last a safe place, of thinking the
past a midden too foul to steep our brains
in. Last week a Dryhope auntie asked me,
"Why remember those nasty centuries
when honest folk were queered, pestered
and malagroozed by clanjamfries of greedy
gangsters who called themselves governments and stock exchanges? I wouldnae
give them headroom."*

*This wish not to see how we got here is
ancient, not modern. Over three hundred
years ago Henry Ford said, "History is
bunk." He was a practical genius who
changed millions of lives by paying folk to
make carriages in big new factories, while
getting millions more to sell and buy
carriages these factories made. Having
mastered the new art of industrial growth
he thought intelligent life needed nothing
else. By 1929 the big new factories had made
more carriages than could be sold at a
profit. The owners closed the factories,
millions of makers lost their jobs and
houses, and even some rich folk suffered.
Ford, not seeing that his method of making*

*money had produced this poverty, blamed
the collapse of industrial housekeeping on
Communists and Jews and said Adolf
Hitler's fascism was the cure. He was partly
right. The Second World War let him
expand his factories again for he used them
to make machines for the American armed
forces. He was not nasty or stupid by nature,
but ignorance of the past fogged his view of
the present and blinded him to the future.*

A History Maker *shows that good states
change as inevitably as bad ones, and
should be carefully watched. My pedantical
lang-nebbed notes at the end try to
emphasize that. They also emulate my son's
modesty by naming me in the third person.
If any future reader learns what happened
to my brave, discontented, kindly, misguided,
long-lost son I hope he or she will add a
postscript for the satisfaction of posterity. I
am sorry that I will not be here to read it.*

*Kate Dryhope
Dryhope Tower
8 December 2234*

ONE

PUBLIC EYE

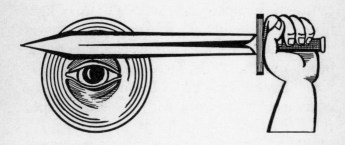

MIST FROM THE SEA covers the hill where a small army lies surrounded by a large. Above the mist and beneath a multitude of stars the public eye hangs like a man-made moon. It is a crystalline globe with lights and appearances of people working in the centre, people whose faces expand hugely when they look outward. They record visions and noises, these people, and comment on them, but now the only noise is the hush-hushing of remote waves breaking on rocks.

The mist slowly brightens to the west where the sun is nearing the horizon. Bugles from under the mist sound a reveille, then come faint scratchings like the noise of many grasshoppers. "The third day of warfare dawns," says the public eye sinking into the mist, "An hour from now the battle for the standard starts."

It pauses among shadowy figures whose activity causes the scratchings. A sudden beam of light from the globe lights a fourteen-year-old boy, haggard and dirty with stained bandages round brow, arm and ankle. He crouches on a cloak which has been his bed. He is sharpening the edge of a short sword with a spindle-shaped stone. The public eye hangs close to his left shoulder. The boy blushes in embarrassment and hones on, pretending not to see until the voice says, "An Ettrick breakfast — not very nourishing."

The boy strikes at the eye with the stone and topples forward on his face.

"A typical reaction," says the eye, skipping sideways and leaving him in darkness, "From one of a hot-headed clan on the verge of extinction. Let us see Northumbria."

The public eye vanishes

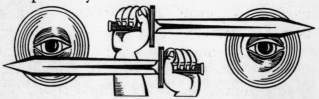

and reappears floating up a slope on the other side of a fog-filled valley. Burners cover the hillside with cheerful dots of light and heat, each surrounded by three soldiers. One unhurriedly sharpens swords, one polishes shields and helmets, a third cooks a breakfast of black puddings fried in their own fat. Those who have prepared their weapons sip mugs of hot coffee laced with rum.

"There is an atmosphere of anticipation," says the public eye, "But anticipation without anxiety, of anticipation tinged with (let us be frank) pleasure. For half a century these doughty Northumbrians have lost brothers, fathers and uncles to Ettrick, so where you and I see the one surviving clan of a gallant Border army the Northumbrians see — and who can blame them? — the remnant of a nest of vipers. Let's hear what the commanders say."

Five Northumbrian commanders stand on a summit, side by side but far enough apart to offer distinct views of themselves. They are old men in their middle thirties with small clipped moustaches, patient, far-seeing expressions and deeply scarred faces. Plain ankle-length cloaks hide their bodies, each with his clan emblem on the left shoulder: the Milburn football, the Storey pencil, the Dodds thunderbolt, the Shafto buckle, the Charlton winged boot. A dawn breeze shreds the mist behind them and reveals five shining steel poles thirty feet high, each topped with a golden eagle gripping a cross beam. From each beam hangs a banner whose slow flappings do not hide the clan emblem on it and the richly embroidered names of past victories.

"How will the battle go today, General Dodds?" says the public eye to the middle commander. Dodds looks at the air over it and speaks as if to himself.

"We'll crush them. They've no food, no water, we outnumber them ten to one. We'll have their standard thirty minutes after starting bell."

"You have lost a lot to Ettrick," says the eye, spinning round Dodds's head to show the wrinkled flesh and small holes where his nose and ears had been.

"More than you see," he replies with a slight smile, "A dad, nine brothers, seven sons, six grandsons, five hands and three legs I've lost. No, nature never meant me for a swordsman. A commander is all I'm fit for and I've never regretted it more than today. I'd love a final chop at Jardine Craig Douglas and his brats."

"How do you think General Craig Douglas managed his campaign, General Dodds?"

"Like a professional. His choice of ground might have led to a draw if Teviot and Liddesdale, Eskdale and Galawater had moved as fast as he moved Ettrick. But they couldn't,

so we've got their standards."
(Here General Shafto gives a loud guffaw which
Dodds ignores.)
"What puzzles me," says Dodds, "Is why he
should make his last stand *there*."
He points a finger across the valley to an
isolated hill now clear of mist. The Ettrick
standard stands on the summit with the remains
of the Ettrick army bivouacked round it. On
every surrounding slope are the bivouacs of
their enemies.
"If Craig Douglas won't surrender — if he's
determined to die for his flag — he could have
found a better den to die in than a waterless
hill where we can come at him from every side."
"Will you invite him to surrender, General
Dodds?"
The commander-in-chief pushes out his under
lip, sucks his moustache and says, "We'll vote
on it. Milburn?"
Milburn says, "He had his last chance yesterday
as far as I'm concerned."
"Give him another," says Storey. Charlton agrees.
"No harm at all in giving old Craig Douglas a
last chance to surrender," says Shafto with
another sharp guffaw, "He won't take it."
"If that's the case, Shafto, you give him the
message," says Dodds, grinning, "Pile it on as
thick as you like, and don't forget the bit about

their aunties."
Shafto nods, salutes and stalks off down the
slope, a herald with a flag of truce striding
beside him. Our point of view remains between
them

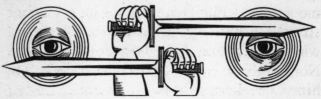

until they ascend the besieged hill as the
Ettrick soldiers gather on the summit. Three
rows of youths, the smallest in front and tallest
behind, stand behind the standard in a crescent
with its tips toward the approaching
Northumbrians. At the foot of the standard
Jardine Craig Douglas is General among his
senior officers. The graceful speed with which
this company has moved into place, the casual
yet energetic stances in which they wait would
seem theatrical to observers used to the
conscript or mercenary troops of the historical
era. Each soldier presents a clear silhouette from
a different angle: arms folded, or thumbs tucked
in belt, or hand on hip and other on sword
hilt. Even the smallest and dirtiest soldier —
he who struck at the public eye with his hone
— has now the poised dignity of a commander
in a painting by Velasquez. Only one lanky

officer slouches near his general like a morose actor who would prefer to be in a different play. General Craig Douglas also has an eccentric aspect. In an epoch when most men are over six feet tall and most generals have neat moustaches Craig Douglas is a gaunt five-foot six whose bushy grey eyebrows, beard and whiskers give him a wild hobgoblin look. The Northumbrian embassy halts three paces before him. The herald blows a fanfare. In the following stillness a lark is heard. Shafto, speaking for all to hear, soon drowns that voice. "Jardine Craig Douglas! I bring a message from Sidney Dodds, commander of Northumbria. You have fought bravely and well — none but your enemies know how well — but today you are doomed unless you surrender that standard, a standard you cannot stop us seizing! You have only a few seasoned troops to defend it and less than a hundred juniors, half of them fledglings. Did you save your youngest blood till last to spill it in a hopeless cause? Surrender now and gladden the hearts of your aunts, sisters and sweethearts. Surrender now and speed the revival of Ettrick as a clan of fighters. Surrender now and lose not one atom of the admiration rightly owed you by the viewing public, your allies, family, enemies and posterity."

"A kind suggestion!" says Craig Douglas swiftly and loudly, "And nobly said. What do you think if it, men? Will we give him that old pole?"

He turns his back on Shafto and stands with fist on hip staring up at the golden eagle above the slowly flapping banner. His question has not been aimed at anyone so nobody replies until he looked sideways at his tallest and most slovenly officer saying, "You are our thinker Wat — you read history books, have been to the stars, have turned down a chance of living forever. What should I do?"

"Give him the pole. Let's go home for a wash and a breakfast," says Wat loudly, "We can order another pole. Our aunts will weave another banner."

"There speaks the voice of reason!" cries Craig Douglas, cheerfully clapping Wat on the shoulder, "The voice of reason and NOT the voice of cowardice as we who fought beside Wat Dryhope yesterday know. But war isnae a reasonable trade."

He moves away from his officers, still staring up at the banner. His voice becomes quieter but more distinct.

"That old pole means a lot to me. I started fighting for it a week before the eldest of you was conceived. We've done well since then. In

battle after battle we've conquered and won
allies until Ettrick has seized standards from
Wick to Barrow and taken some on commons
as far south as Sunningdale. But today Ettrick
is the only undefeated clan on the Scottish
Borders — one hundred and eight of us, mostly
cadets and fledglings — one hundred and eight
hungry, thirsty folk surrounded by over a
thousand experienced, well-watered, well-fed
warriors. So my good son Wat says, 'Drop the
pole. Give them the flag. They'll take it anyway.
Nobody will blame us.' That is reasonable
advice and I reject it!"

He flings his right hand toward the flag crying,
"That flag flew over us in the bonny days when
we were many and strong. Will we abandon it
now just because we are few and weak? Have
we become so sensible — so comfortable — so
unmanly that we can bask like lions in the
sunlight of victory but flee like hens from the
shadow of certain death? A heroic defeat makes
brave men as glorious as a victory I think!"

He points upward at the public eye which floats
round the standard between him and his
crescent of soldiers, but he looks to them as he
declares, "There is the eye which will show the
world how the Ettrick clan will die, will show
your sweethearts and aunts how their men can
die! I ask you to die with me so that our death

will be viewed and viewed again to the last days
of mankind and television and time! Is anybody
with me?"
As nearly everyone draws breath to roar their
support Wat yells, "Stop and listen! Listen to
me!"

All stare at him. The public eye draws near.
With a gesture which tries to dismiss it he says,
"Yes Dad, we fight to show our contempt for
death but we old ones have done that more than
once. Remember the bairns, the fourteen-year-
olds! This is their first war. Give them the
chance of another. Send them home."
"Thanks for reminding me," says Craig
Douglas walking into the crescent of troops
behind the standard, "Let the fledglings he
speaks about take one step forward."
In the front rank some lads glance sideways at
each other but none move their feet.
"Come," he says kindly, "Ye cannae hide from
me! Charlie and Jimmy, you're fourteen — I
know my sons' ages. And Sandy, Kenneth, and
Alec are my kin among the Bowerhopes. Step
forward, loons, or I'll command each of ye
singly. An auld bitch like me cannae have
mutinous pups."
Twenty boys shuffle forward. He smiles and
says, "You were bairns when I brought ye into

battle two days since. Now you are warriors. This is my last order for you. Go behind the Northumbrian lines with General Shafto. Return to your aunts. When your wounds heal join the veterans and Boys' Brigade in the Warrior house where you will be the only officers. Review this war from start to finish. Learn from our mistakes. Teach the Ettrick youngsters how to avoid them. Prepare future victories to avenge the losses of today. Away with ye!"

Still the boys keep their places, some looking sideways at each other, some staring doggedly ahead. One raises a hand.

"Aye, Charlie?" says the General.

"Do you think . . . if we fight beside ye . . . we'll let Ettrick down, Dad?"

"I doubt it, Charlie."

A renewed silence is broken by an older boy in the rear.

"Permission to speak Uncle."

"Granted."

"The young loons ken the laws of democratic warfare as well as we. You were elected to lead us in battle. You cannae order men to retreat unless their wounds or characters make them encumbrances."

"I agree," says Craig Douglas gently, "Step back those who choose to die with the rest of us."

The youngsters step back.

"I tried, Wat," says the General, sighing and strolling to the standard, "But all my fledglings have turned into eagles. Will *you* leave me now?"

"You're a waster, Dad," said Wat glumly, "An arrogant feckless blood-crazy waster. But I cannae live alone among the women."

"So I have reason on my side after all!" shouts Craig Douglas with a laugh. Everyone but Wat echoes it. Even Shafto and the herald are laughing.

"General Shafto," says Craig Douglas in a voice cutting the laughter short, "Thank Sidney Dodds and say we will meet his men —" (he glances at his wristcom) "— in nine minutes."

"Good!" says Shafto, grinning. He salutes and strides back down the hill with the herald. The public eye remains.

"Mibby I'm a waster, but I'm not feckless when it comes to strategy," Craig Douglas tells his army, "We cannae win this fight, but we won't lose it if you do what I say. I and Joe Dryhope will take the rear guard, Colonel Wardlaw the right wing, Archie Elphinstone the left. Wat leads the van with three picked men who take their cues from him. The outcome depends on that . . . No spying! This collogue is private," he tells the public eye. It soars upward while the Ettricks pull on their helmets and form a circle.

The public eye is now so high above the standard that hill and moorland and armed companies are spread beneath like a map with streams of ants pouring across.

"Four minutes from now the massacre of the decade begins," says a voice. "The day is mild and dry, visibility good, the ground in fine condition. General Craig Douglas said he has a strategy which will prevent defeat. What can it be, Wolfgang Hochgeist?"

"I cannot possibly say," says another voice, "For I do not think it can be done. The remark was, I fear, a nervous one. The nervous Craig Douglas nature appears in all males of that blood, especially in Wat Dryhope, the General's eldest son."

"So what can Craig Douglas do?"

"He can form a compact mass round the standard and fight on the spot till the last man drops, but too many of his soldiers are children for such a Teutonic stand. The Scottish temper *and* steepness of the hill indicate a downhill charge toward a more defensible standpoint.

There are three: Blind Ghyll Quarry half a mile
to the west; a windbreak wood to the south;
and to the east, where the sea cliffs descend to
an old atomic power station, the most tempting
standpoint of all — a long concrete jetty in
good condition. If the standard could be got
there a troop of forty might hold off a thousand
till nightfall, but Dodds commands five armies
and has held back three to block approaches to
the jetty, quarry and wood."

"The Ettricks are unpegging the guy ropes of
their standard!" cries the other voice. "Where
they aim it when lowered will give a clue. Here
comes the umpire!"

A white airship appears between clouds
overhead, a red cross on the side and fifty small
aircraft fixed to the underside. From a porthole
comes a vivid flash then the clang of an
enormous bell. The Ettricks stay in a tight mass
round their standard on the hilltop. Three
columns of Northumbrians approach the hill
from different sides and start climbing to the
top in curving paths that leave no straight
opening for the force on the summit to charge
through. The company on the summit regroup
round their standard which dips to horizontal.
Ropes, banner are swiftly twisted round the
pole, it becomes the spine of a central column

with a short column in front, longer ones on each side and behind. Dodds's vanguard is nearing the summit when the Ettricks charge from it and crash like a torpedo through Shafto's column.

"Where are they going? Where are they going? Where *are* they going?" demands the public eye at an altitude which keeps the whole field of action in view. Among the soldiers below other eyes record the bloody strife of individual bodies. "To the jetty by way of the cliff," says Hochgeist, "But it is too far, much too far away for them! Hopeless!"

"Yet most of Ettrick have passed through Shafto's men with surprisingly few losses and now run into Milburn's ranks like a knife into butter! Dodds's men on the hilltop are breaking formation and pouring down after them like an avalanche. The best the Ettricks can do is let their heels defend them. Their central column has gained the bottom of the slope and now pushes by the shortest way to the cliff top, why? They can't mean to pitch their standard into the sea?"

"Indeed no," says Hochgeist, "Their last ten victories would be discounted by the War Council in Geneva. Craig Douglas may wish his clan to perish on this promontory for sentimental reasons. I believe the Picts made a historic stand here once."

"But his clan will be wiped out before they reach it! Craig Douglas turns with his rear guard to face the enemy and now he's really in the thick of it! What a man! Look at the action of that sword! But the Northumbrians are overwhelming him while the rest chase and surround the Ettrick standard which is shedding its defenders like an onion shedding skins yet fighting and thrusting upward all the time with Wat Dryhope in the lead! And they've reached it — the cliff edge — what are they trying to do? Are they actually raising the standard for a last flap of the old flag?"
"Aha!"
"There's hardly a dozen left!"
"Aha!"
"Why *won't* they surrender that damned pole? What are they trying to do, Wolfgang?"
"Something very clever which has never been done before and which only a hopelessly outnumbered force in exactly this cliff-edge situation could achieve. I have underrated Craig Douglas. What a pity he did not live to see his plan carried through. But his nervous son may actually succeed."

The Ettrick standard, wagging like a corn stalk in a gale, is planted a yard from the cliff edge by its last few defenders. Wat holds the

pole while landward of him three youngsters
grasp ropes which stop it toppling into the sea.
An Ettrick remnant hack and thrust to hold
back a Northumbrian throng whose main wish
is now to grab these very ropes.

"Get a hold before you kill them!" screams
Dodds from the rear.

"Now!" yells Wat. At once the ropes are flung aside
and grasped by Northumbrian hands. The pole
too has been released to a Northumbrian. Wat
stands a pace away, eyeing him. There is a pause.

"You surrender?" screams Dodds from the rear.
Soldiers round the standard, Ettrick and
Northumbrian, stare at Wat whose great height
and sudden composure make him seem the only
man fit to answer. Though bruised and bloody
he no longer looks clumsy. With a goblinish
grin he shouts, "No!" and lunges at the
Northumbrian holding the pole.

"The Ettrick survivors now assault the
Northumbrians holding their standard!" says
Hochgeist. "Though hopelessly outnumbered
the surprise of their attack in this narrow space
has made the four or five Northumbrians
holding the ropes release them and . . . OVER
SHE GOES!"

    The public eye takes in a picture to be
replayed in slow motion for centuries to come:

a toppling steel pole tipped with an eagle, a
flame-like banner unrolling behind like the tail
of a comet, both going down toward the
wrinkled blue-grey silk of the North Sea, then
striking it obliquely and passing under with a
splash. Half of the silvery length shoots up
again at an angle then the whole length settles
and finally sinks.

"Was that allowed by the rules?"

"I think so, yes," says Hochgeist, laughing,
"Because the rules do not forbid it. The
Northumbrians captured the standard in fair
fight. It was they who let it fall in the sea after
an Ettrick counter-attack in a battle which still
continues."

"Yes the Northumbrians have gone berserk,"
says the public eye. "It's an ugly sight, but who
can blame them? After half a century of victories
Clan Ettrick has drawn on a technicality so even
if the entire Ettrick army is exterminated it
retires unbeaten. Exterminated it will certainly
be unless — good! There goes the bell for end
of play. And now as the Red Cross aircraft
descend on the field of honour some of you
may want to switch to the banks of the Alamo
for a peep at the big fight between the Tex and
Mex sharpshooters; but I know many will stay
with us here to learn the final body-count as
the medicals get down to business."

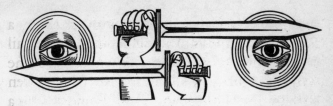

The Northumbrian to whom he released the standard was the first man Wat Dryhope had deliberately killed. In previous fights his blows had been dealt in the thick of things, as much for defence as aggression, but his lunge at the Northumbrian had not been parried. His sword pierced a heart below a bewildered face because his victim had thought the battle over. Weary and disgusted Wat fell to the ground, saw the standard topple past him, heard renewed screams and yelling. Wanting no more he rolled over the cliff edge after the standard and lost consciousness.

Later he saw seagulls far beneath pecking at something in the waves. For a while he thought he was looking down on his drowned body. Aches in every muscle soon dismissed that idea. He was dangling on the cliff-face over a partly solid and partly yielding projection. When his hands gripped it sharp spines jagged the palms and fingers. He groaned but held tight, trying to turn sideways.

"Is this the last of the Ettricks?" asked a face in

a globe three inches from his nose.

"Fuck off," he muttered, then yelled it with the full force of his lungs.

"Wat Dryhope, eldest son of the slaughtered general," said the face, "And clearly a reader who likes the robust language of twentieth-century fiction."

"Hello, can I give you a hand?" asked another voice. Wat wrenched himself round and saw grey rock split by horizontal cracks. His torso lay on a clump of whins rooted in a crack above a narrow ledge. Twisting his face upward he saw the cliff top a few feet above with a figure kneeling on the edge. It was General Shafto, stretching an arm down and saying, "Come on — let's have you."

Wat raised a bloodstained right hand whose fingers, he knew, could now hold nothing, but Shafto gripped the wrist and dragged Wat up and over the edge as he fainted again.

He wakened a minute later with the neck of a flask between his teeth and a mouthful of burning fluid which set him spluttering.

"My aunts say this stuff does more harm than good," said Shafto taking a swig, "I don't believe them."

"Thanks," said Wat and propped himself up on an elbow. Judging by the sun less than an hour had passed since Ettrick had lowered the standard and charged downhill, yet the only signs of battle on the moorland slopes were some gangrels collecting scattered swords, helmets, shields of the dead and badly maimed. Three or four groups of Northumbrians stood or sprawled in small groups awaiting transport. Departing trucks in the distance showed where the rest had gone. The hospital ship still hung between clouds overhead; all dead and wounded bodies except his own had been lifted into it. A Red Cross aircraft was settling on the ground a hundred yards away; he saw nurses with a stretcher preparing to come for him.

"You were lucky it was me and not old Dodds who found you," said Shafto affably, "He'd have pushed you into the sea. He says you got that draw by a trick — a filthy trick."

"He's right. Attacking after pretending to surrender is warfare for weans. When Dad gave his orders we were too feart and excited to think."

"You'll feel better when the medics have put more blood back into you," said Shafto, "Your dad was a genius. He saw a loophole in the rules and made it work for him. People are tired of the old strategies — that battle will be disked by millions. In a month or three you and me should put our heads together and see if we can work out other new strategies — within the Geneva Conventions of course, always within the Conventions. I want you for an ally one day."

As Wat was carried to the aircraft he said harshly, "Am I the last? Are all the rest of Ettrick dead?"
"No no no!" said a nurse soothingly, "Fourteen are living and most of them can be mended. Your brother Joe will mend."
"Good," said Wat and wept, covering his face with his hands. The public eye floated above it saying, "Goodbye Wat Dryhope, a hero of our time — a brave, nervous, tricky hero obviously shaken to the core by what may be eventually voted The Battle of The Century, a surprising last-minute draw between Ettrick and the five clans of Northumbria United."

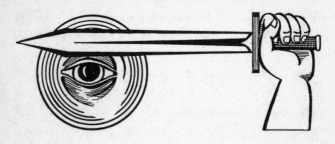

TWO

PRIVATE HOUSES

THE RED CROSS put the dead soldiers into pure white vaults below their homes where useless things were made good again. Women who had most loved them washed the bodies, laying them neatly between their belongings and the weapons and armour returned by the gangrels. Later the whole family came down for a last visit. Sisters, nieces, aunts wept and clasped each other. Children mooned around looking woeful or puzzled until grannies helped them choose an instrument, ornament or video to remind them of a favourite brother or uncle. The living left and the vault was sealed. Clear liquid welled from the floor until it covered everything inside. The liquid turned black and frothy like Irish stout, sank back through the floor into the roots of the powerplant and left the vault perfectly empty and clean.

On the day after the funeral a morning service was held in the stalk room of Dryhope house. Smooth, milk-white and six feet wide the stalk grew like a tree from the floor and out through the ceiling. All who remained of the family were gathered round it except three members of the Boys' Brigade: these were at the Warrior house watching replays of the recent war with other junior cadets. In a few days they would return with solemn faces and expectations of being more thoroughly served by women, but now their sisters, aunts and grannies sprawled, reclined or squatted about the floor on rugs and large cushions. The four greatest great-grandmothers were enthroned in chairs. The only two adult males also had raised seats. Joe, smoking a good cigar, lay in a wheelchair with attachments supporting the stumps of an arm and leg. Wat, lightly bandaged, sprawled on a chaise longue.

A stately woman of fifty was mother that day and stood at a crystalline table, the top patterned with coloured points of light which flowed from her finger-tips and continually changed as she played a *Sanctus* which had preceded the miracle of transubstantiation for centuries before. The *Sanctus* ended and two sturdy girls of twelve stood facing her, one on each side of the stalk. Silencing the organ she attended to the orders of the day. Nurses asked for flasks of cell serum and protein to help the growth of Joe's new arm and leg, an ointment to ease Granny Tibs's rheumatic knee, and Elastoplast for the medical chest. The mother struck the organ. With a low humming the objects appeared as diagrams on the stalk, each inside a circle. There were clicks, twangs and gurgles as the outlines received colour and tone. With sharp detonations the images became solid things in round cavities. The acolytes lifted them out and gave them to the nurses. With heavy thuds the cavities became grey blotches which faded from the stalk leaving it an unblemished, delicate shade of palest pink. The mother had made the sound sequence easier on the ear by blending it with chords from the *Agnus Dei* by Carver, Palestrina, Bach and Berlioz, covering the last thuds with a loud Amen which faded with the blotches fading from the stalk.

Then the teachers ordered disks, paper, pencils, paint; the cooks milk, cheese, flour, sugar, coffee beans; the henwife ordered a sack of meal, a sack of corn, a first edition of Lindsay's *Voyage to Arcturus*; the joiner ordered parts for a new orthopaedic bed she was making for Joe; weavers and embroiderers asked for many different colours of yarn and silk. When all were delivered the stalk was flushed rose red, a throbbing was heard from the underground roots and the room was colder, sure signs of plant exhaustion.

" A light order now," said the mother. "Granny Tibs?"

Granny Tibs was one hundred and twenty and ordered a doll for her two-year-old great-great-great-great-great-granddaughter. It had to be exactly like a doll she remembered playing with herself at that age, a china girl doll with curly yellow hair, blue eyes, a matching silk dress with a big bow at the back. When the diagram appeared she remembered that the hair had not been curly but smooth, and twisted in two long plaits tied with bows at the ends. The dress had also been of a historical kind called *dirndl* worn by the women of Bolivia or California — that should be a clue — the dress was illustrated in a book called *Heidi Grows Up* which had been published she thought in the eighteenth or perhaps nineteenth century. The doll was also made of cloth, not china at all. It took a long time to get exactly the doll Granny Tibs remembered and by then the colour of the stalk and temperature of the room were normal again. The children now spoke out. A young jeweller wanted two hundred grammes of silver wire and was persuaded to accept a hundred of copper. A young sculptor who asked for six kilogrammes of clay was told to collect it from Mountbenger where some aunts had a pottery; she said she hated Mountbenger because of a boy there, so was given a four-page geological guide to help her find her own supply of clay. A very young wood-worker wanted a sharp new chisel but the joiner said she would show him how to sharpen his old one. This answer caused outcries which the mother drowned with a blast of cheery sound.

Finally she faced the men and said, "Cigars, Joe?"

"I've all I need, Auntie," he answered, blowing a smoke ring. She said, "Wat, you have a wanting look."

"Have I? Then give me something that stops memories."

"You can have Paxil, Zoloft, or Prozac, Gilbey's London gin, The Macallan, Courvoisier or a thousand other derivatives of alcohol, opium and cocaine."

"I want nothing that changes my chemistry,"

he said coldly, "Give me a history book — not
a statistical one — a book that reads like
somebody talking."

"What period?"

"A period of excitement when folk thought they
were making a better world."

Only the mother looked straight at Wat but a
new alertness in the room seemed shared by
everyone except the boys, the oldest great-
granny, Kittock the henwife and, apparently,
Joe.

"There were many such times," said the mother.
She pressed the organ and a table of names and
dates flowed onto the stalk.

"The foundation of Israel, A.D. or B.C.?" she
suggested, "The rise of Islam? Children's
Crusade? Peasants' Revolt? French Revolution?
More books have been written about each than
there are brands of alcohol."

There was a silence in which Wat reddened with
embarrassment. Everyone seemed to be
watching him. A calm, monotonous yet oddly
sing-song voice said, "Have you read *Ten Days
That Shook the World*, Wat?"

Kittock the henwife had spoken without lifting
her eyes from the novel on her lap.

"Never," said Wat thankfully.

"Well, that's the book for you."

So Wat ordered *Ten Days That Shook the*

World, Reed's account of Muscovite politics
in 1917. The plant substantiated it. A girl gave
it to him.

"Come outside, Wat" said Joe setting his chair
in motion, "I need to see some hills."

Wat started following but paused when the
mother said, "Wat, you have lost a father,
brothers, friends. We have lost brothers, lovers
and sons in a war we never wanted."

"I pity you of course," said Wat, shrugging,
"But a circus will be here in a few days. Men
will be coming from all over Scotland and even
farther. Make the most of them."

He strode out.

On this sunny spring day the projecting eaves
of Dryhope house neatly shadowed the
surrounding veranda. Joe sat here watching the
view with the intense frown of a starving man
who cannot quite believe in the meal before
him. From under the veranda a flow of pure
water fed a series of pools linked by waterfalls.
The nearest held trout and cresses and a marble
bird-table shaped like a twentieth-century
aircraft carrier. The second was a play-pool

where infants splashed and shouted in sight of two ten-year-old aunts who lay gossiping on a nearby lawn. The third was a fishpond in a vegetable garden stretching all round the house. The last was a duckpond from which Dryhope burn flowed down through a glen planted with fruit trees and berry bushes. On the right bank stood Dryhope Tower, an ancient keep used by the henwife. A steepening of the hillside hid land immediately beyond but not Saint Mary's Loch half a mile away. Today the calm surface exactly reflected the high surrounding hills with woods of pine, oak, birk, rowan, reflected also three houses by the shore. Oxcleuch, Cappercleuch and Bowerhope resembled Dryhope: large, low-walled, broad-eaved mansions, each with the slim white inverted cone of a powerplant stalk growing dim and invisible after the first hundred feet. The summits appeared at cloud level, each a disc of bright vapour from which a line of vapour flowed east with the wind. More than fifty such discs patterned the sky. The remotest over powerplants in Moffat, Eskdale and Teviot, looked like tiny flecks in the wedges of blue air between the hills. Lines of vapour from these and many more in the west ruled the heavenly blue into parallel strips. The lines were more emphatic today, as always after big funerals.

Joe pointed to the view with his only foot and said wistfully, "There's a lot of goodness out there."

"But ye cannae feel it," said Wat, who sat cross-legged and reading on a rug beside him.

"No yet."

"Maybe you'll never feel part of that goodness again. I lost the feeling with my first battle."

"Pessimist. I'm no like you. I'll feel as good as ever when I get back my arm and leg."

Joe glanced wistfully down at the crystalline cylinders extending from his right shoulder and right thigh. Tiny atomic motors among the pinkish-brown broth inside were nudging together cells of new limbs, but a month would pass before outlines of bones appeared. Joe sighed then said, "You made them very tense in there. You should keep ill-sounding words for me or the Warrior house."

"Dryhope women are stupid," said Wat coldly, "They think I'm mourning the Dad — that daft old prick."

"It should be possible for you to mourn the Dad," said Joe gently, "*I'm* mourning him and he loved you most, loved you more than anyone because you're our bonniest fighter and always argle-bargled with him. He liked contention. Are you mourning the bairns?"

"Rage not sorrow is my disease. Why did our

fucking old progenitor con nearly all Ettrick
into dying round a pole with a tin chicken on
top? Why did he want us to fight after the
decent chiefs of Teviot and Eskdale, Liddesdale
and Galawater had surrendered? I'll tell you
why. He was past his prime and knew he was
fighting his last war. He wanted to take our
whole army into the roots with him. Our bairns
were slaughtered because our Dad feared age
and loneliness."

"He made sure we'll be remembered! The lot
of us! Living and dead!" said Joe with a small
firm smile, "The bairns too, in fact the bairns
most of all. 'All my fledglings have turned into
eagles,' he said. O he was right. Wee lads of
fourteen have never chosen to die like that
before — not since the dawn of television. If
history wasnae a thing of the past I would say
Ettrick *made it* two days ago. The strategy was
the Dad's but only you had the spunk to get
the standard to the cliff top and kill the man
you passed it to . . . What's wrong?"

"I'm remembering his face," muttered Wat after
a moment. He had dropped his book and was
biting his nails. Joe said softly, "A cigar?" and
offered one.

"No."

After a minute of silence Joe said mildly,

"You're wrong about Dad wanting us all to go out with him. He saved me by falling on me when Dodds's butchers were hacking us both, that was no accident. But nothing you say upsets me, Wat — you arenae normal. You're a hero. I'm proud of what you did. And I don't care if all this . . . " (he waved his only hand at the view) " . . . never seems sweet to me again. Pride will keep me going, like it keeps you."

He looked down at Wat who was reading again, or pretending to. Joe said, "How can a soldier who thinks our last war too bloody forget it by reading about dark ages when men fought wars without rules, and burned bombed looted peaceful houses, and killed raped enslaved whole families of women children and old ones — and boasted about it in their filthy newspapers! I hated history when I was wee. When Granny Pringle showed us films from those days I had nightmares."

"I'm reading about folk who struggled to stop all that," said Wat, "They were the greatest heroes."

"Well, mibby, but it was the powerplants that stopped all that."

For a while the only sounds were sparrows twittering on the bird table, infant shouts and splashes, a dull distant boom from Oxcleuch where something metallic was being synthesized. Joe said, "How would you like to die, Wat, if not in a battle folk would replay for centuries?"

"By heart failure while weeding a cabbage patch."

"Aye, only dafties despise gardening," said Joe thoughtfully, "But soldiers like us have no patience for it."

Wat pocketed his book and stood up.

"You're no fool, Joe," he said, "You're also brave, honest and good-natured so you'll be our next general."

"Me? General Joe of Ettrick? Why not General Wat?" said Joe grinning shyly, "You're our hero."

"I'm moody — a Hamlet type — good for sudden sprints and useless in the long run. I'll go now."

"Aye, a ride will help ye relax. Arrange one for me."

Wat went down to the lawn, showed the larger of the little aunts his bandaged palms and said politely, "Lend me your hands Auntie Jean, these arenae much use."

She jumped happily up and trotted beside him through an orchard with beehives under the trees. They entered a stable with a backdoor onto the common on the far side of the deer fence and went through it, collecting saddle, bridle, sugar lumps and whistle from the tackroom. On the common several horses grazed within sight of a water trough.

"I need an experienced old pony," said Wat, "Sophia will do."

He blew three notes on the whistle. A sedate dapple grey with long main and tail moved nearer without ceasing to crop grass.

"I know where you're going! I know where you're going!" shouted Auntie Jean excitedly. Wat threw the saddle onto the pony, offered it sugar and held the head while Jean's strong little hands slipped on the bridle and tightened buckles on that and the girths. Wat inspected the buckles, set foot in stirrup, thrust most of himself over the pony's back and with some groaning arrived upright in the saddle.

"I'll lead you!" shouted Jean skipping about, "I'll lead you to all the randy aunties of Craig Douglas!"

"You willnae," said Wat, "Give me those."

With a pout of annoyance she handed up the reins. He gripped them clumsily with his thumbs and said, "You don't know where I'm

going, Jean. Clap her and goodbye."
Jean turned the pony to face east and downhill
and clapped her rump. Sophia, liking her rider,
set off briskly although he turned her uphill
and north.

By easy slopes he headed for Hawkshaw Rig
but later turned right into a glen between that
and Wardlaw, then crossed a fast-flowing burn
and descended into woods behind Craig
Douglas house, hoping to enter the grounds
unseen. He failed. The backdoor in the deer
fence banged open as he neared and four boys
ran out, jostling for priority in helping him
dismount and stable Sophia.
"If Jean clyped on me she's a sleekit wee bitch,"
he told them. They said nothing. Leaving the
stable for the garden he saw all the Craig
Douglas children and adolescents standing to
left and right of the path, staring. Even babies
in the arms of older sisters were gazing at him
in silent wonder. He paused and said, "When I
last came here you were a lot noisier."
Nobody spoke.
"Have you no tale for me Annie?" he asked a
tall girl with a humorous cast of features. She
said faintly, "We're glad you've no come back
like our uncles, Wat."
He shrugged, went on to the house and found

a mother waiting on the veranda. A week before she had been pleasantly plump; now there were dark hollows under her cheekbones and red-rimmed eyes. He said gruffly, "You look twenty years older, Mirren."

She said coldly, "You're the same as ever. Have you come to see your pals?"

He thought for a moment. The outer walls of the house and most of the inner ones were transparent just now. Only the dark-walled infirmary and the room of the woman he wanted to see allowed no glimpse of their interior. He sighed and nodded.

And followed the mother inside and across floors where only young women looked straight at him. Grannies, matrons and even a girl suckling an infant ignored him or looked away: this disturbed him far more than the silence of the youngsters outside. He was brought into the infirmary where five big translucent boxes lay, each containing what seemed pink fog with a complicated shadow inside. The mother pressed a stud. The infirmary darkened but the shadows became the well-lit bodies of young, naked, badly dismembered men, each with limbs and organs floating beside their torso and linked to it by threads like cobwebs. Only one body exhibited movement: eyes which slowly

blinked in time with a mouth opening and
shutting like the mouth of a fish. The face had
no intelligence in it. Wat abruptly turned his
back on these things. The ceiling went clear
and admitted sunlight again.

"You can mend them?" he asked in a voice shrill
with unbelief.

"Mibby. Perhaps. It will take years but they're
just lads."

"Mirren, most of Charlie's head is gone."

"He'll grow a new one if we can restore the
heart. The new brain will have his character if
not his memories."

"Our memories *are* our character, Mirren."

"Then the mother and sisters who love him will
restore his memories, Wat Dryhope. We'll give
him back all the good things the war sliced
away, but *you* won't be one of them, Wattie!
When he starts thinking again we'll only remind
him of what's harmless!"

"You're so maddened by grief that you're
blethering, Mirren. I know it's a cruel injustice
that I'm almost unhurt and your lads are nearly
dead, but I'm the man who argued for what
would have saved them. They refused it. And
have you forgot that bloody Daddy Jardine was
born and bred in this house by Craig Douglas
women? Our general's obstrapulous conceit
wasnae nourished by the aunties of Dryhope."

"No woman on earth nourished Jardine's conceit!" cried Mirren, "He got it in the Warrior house. *We* never scorned him for his wee-ness but other soldiers did until he showed he was spunkier than them and could take knocks without squealing. So they made him their pet, then elected him boss, and after that Craig Douglas never saw him again — except through the public eye — until two days back when the Red Cross gave us his remains with sixteen other corpses and the pieces you're feart to turn round and see. Women had no part in making a bloody hero of Jardine Craig Douglas. Yes, he fathered weans in half the houses along Yarrow but he only wanted women for one thing. Like all soldiers the only folk he really loved were men!"

Wat heard this with bowed head then said, "All true, Aunt Mirren, but women arenae wholly innocent of the war game. You don't take to fighting like we do — the world holds hardly a dozen tribes of professional Amazons — but many girls, aye, and many women are daft about soldiers. I'm a graceless brute so when I came home from the stars few women outside Dryhope house would look at me — not until I fought for Ettrick and showed some talent."

"I cannae be fair to you, Wat," the mother said drying her eyes, "Go to Nan."

He walked swiftly to the other opaque-walled room, looking ceilingward to avoid eye-contact with anyone before reaching it. A teenage girl scampered out as he was about to enter, followed by another. He went in and shut the door by pulling across a heavy tapestry curtain. Then he faced the woman inside and said, "See me Nan! I'm a rare animal now, an Ettrick warrior with nothing obvious missing. But I cannae move my fingers and I feel nine tenths dead and as sexless as a neep. Do you still like Wat Dryhope?"

She smiled and beckoned.

Next morning she wakened Wat by prizing his arms from around her and saying, "You neednae hold so tight, I won't run away."

She slipped out of bed and pulled on a long loose shirt. He raised himself by an elbow to watch. Playing a keyboard invisible to him she made a clear round window in the wall before her and raised it until it framed a hawk perched on the top branch of a Scotch pine and the summit of Whitelaw against a pale sky. By light from this Nan opened elegant boxes holding the materials of a meal and made breakfast.

She was nearly forty with short dark hair and a lively, clever face which appreciated everything she saw. While poaching an egg her frown of concentration left a small smile at the corners of the mouth, a humorous look which had been inherited by her daughters. Nearby was a loom where she wove rugs, door curtains, pillows with patterns that made this room different from any other, also the screen she used to design new patterns or play music. She had a talent for every worthwhile art, handling utensils with swift ease which soothed Wat's mind as much as her fingers had soothed the rest of him the night before. He said, "I want to stay with you, here, in this room, till all the seas run dry, my dear, and the rocks melt in the sun. Can I do it for a week or two?"

"War fatigue?" she said, looking hard at him.

"No. I'm afraid of news from Geneva."

"Are you feart they'll disqualify the draw with Northumbria?"

"No. *I hope* they disqualify that draw. It will discourage suicidal heroics that have become the bane of honest warfare, especially in Scotland."

"Then what are you afraid of?"

"Did ye see our last battle?"

"Certainly not. No decent woman who's borne a son watches battles."

Slowly, almost unwillingly, Wat told her that someone he knew had struck a blow which had the appearance of being foul and might be condemned as such.

"Who was that?" said Nan, looking at Wat more closely still.

"If Geneva condemns him you'll soon know," said Wat drearily, "If it doesnae I'll try to forget about it. Let me stay here for a fortnight Nan."

She said firmly, "Not possible. An hour from now I become mother and I cannae mother a whole household with you waiting round to be served. Sit up."

She placed a closed mug of coffee where his mouth could reach a tube sticking from the top, then she sat on the bedside with a plate on her lap and fed him slices of poached-egg-on-toast. She said, "Go to Annie's room — she's mad about you and has no responsibilities. Stay there as long as you like. It will teach her something. Craig Douglas needs more bairns now and *I* don't want to carry another."

He groaned and said, "I think of Annie as a wee sister."

"Aye, because you never look at her. Do it. Dick

Megget was her dad. The Meggets havenae fucked with Dryhopes for three generations, there's no fear of incest."

He said wistfully, "With you, in this room, I feel better, more sure of myself than anywhere else in the world."

"I doubt it. Annie says you looked bloody sure of yourself in that last battle. She plays it six times a day. She says you're magnificent. Why are you no magnificent with me?"

He scowled. She said, "Cheer up! You were my favourite soldier long before the rest got chopped. I liked you most *because* you didnae act the big hero. Yet in battle you're better than others. Why?"

"Easy told," said Wat drearily, "I'm usually clumsier than other men because I don't like life as much, so danger speeds this body without upsetting this brain. Most soldiers only enjoy battles when looking back on them — while fighting they're too excited to think so do it automatically. I think cooler and hit faster while fighting so I enjoy it at the time. Afterward the memory depresses me. I wish I had another talent."

"I remember you six years ago as a queer lanky clever lad who wanted to seed the stars and got accepted for it. Were you useless there?"

"No, I could do the work but I hated the narrow

places in the satellites, hated that every gramme of air we breathed or green thing we looked on had been contrived by human skill. I didnae hate it all, of course. A good thing about satellites is their lack of nourishment for our kind of powerplant, so men and women earn their living room by working together as equals. The men have no time for warfare. They sometimes fight duels, but hardly ever to the death. Many couples live as husband and wife and think of earthmen as lazy lecherous belligerent primitives. I agreed with them but I couldnae stand the enclosed spaces they lived in. Anyway, for me the satellites were just stepping-stones to the universe where immortals are making new worlds — and I hated that universe most of all. I could hardly face the deserts of dead rock and frozen stoor between the domed craters. The stars are fearsome out there, white, steady, and intense. Look at any two of them and if, like me, you're cursed with good sight, you soon see a hundred between. Look hard at any two of those and the same thing happens no matter how close they seem. I lost all sense of darkness between them. It was not the vast darkness but the endless lights, the millions of starlights that made me feel less than a grain of stoor myself — I felt like zero. I trudged across one of these

deserts with Groombridge who was testing my
fitness for immortality. He said immortality
would madden me unless I had a good reason
for it and the only good reason was in the grains
of dirt under our boots, the millions of stars
over our helmets. He said the silence of these
spaces did not appal minds in the network
conspiring to bring them to life, but
generations of mortals would die and be
forgotten before Mars, Venus and the moons
of Jupiter and Saturn had the ground and air
to support freely evolving plants and
intelligences. This was why people who chose
immortality must prepare to live almost
completely in the future. The main difference
between *neo-sapience* and *proto-sapience*
(that is what immortals call themselves and us)
is, that the longer neo-sapiences live the more
they know of their future, the longer we live
the more we know of our past. Groombridge
said mortals cling harder to the past as they
age, so our lives have a tragic sweetness neo-
sapience lacks, a painful sweetness got from
memories of lost childhood, lost love, lost
friends, lost opportunities, lost beauty et cetera
— lost *life*, in other words. He said, 'Our
rejuvenation treatment still retains an
embarrassing wealth of early memories but in
two or three centuries we'll overcome that. If

you become immortal, Mr. Dryhope, by your five thousandth year the first fifty will have been erased by more recent, more urgent, more useful experiences, most of them gained through a virtual keyboard and scanner or their future equivalent. By your five thousandth year it is possible — and by your five millionth inevitable — that you will work in another galaxy in a body whose form we cannot now predict. By then, of course, the planet of your origin, like a myriad other worlds you've helped reshape, will have ceased to be even a cipher in your calculations. Perhaps I repel you, Mr. Dryhope?' Yes, he scunnered me like a creature I once saw in an aquarium. It was harmless but I couldnae watch it because it breathed, ate and ejaculated through holes which, to my mind, were in the wrong places. From feeling zero he had made me feel minus, an absence with an ache inside. I had to return to things as bonny and temporary as you and those."

He pointed to the green hilltop and the bird on the branch, then began biting his nails. She stopped that by putting down the plate and kissing him.

Later she washed, dried and dressed him in clean garments saying, "Don't play the helpless wean too much with Annie, she's had none of her own. Your hands will soon heal if you work the fingers."

He said, "Nan, is there a kind, experienced body in Craig Douglas who would visit my brother Joe who's short of an arm and leg? Three of his other limbs are in working order — four if you count the tongue."

Nan said she would consider this.

"And Nan," he muttered, looking away from her, "There is no kinder or more experienced body in Craig Douglas than you, but please get someone else to go."

She stared, laughed then said, "Mibby you would have been happier in the bad old historical days when it was a man's duty to be jealous, but I doubt it."

Survivors of great slaughters knew they must help the women of their clan replace lost comrades so duty, not desire brought Wat to Annie's room. Apart from a homo-erotic affair in the Warrior house all Wat's lovers until now had been older than him so the childish furnishing in Annie's room almost made him walk away. Shelves were crowded with cuddly toys, romantic videos about historical lovers and comic ones about talking animals. A typical young girl's collage covered the walls; it showed Annie in many moods and dresses from babyhood to teens mingled with pictures of her mother, aunts, grannies, pets, girl friends, boyfriends and popular icons. Wat recognized Donald Duck, Botticelli's Venus, Robert Burns, Alice in Wonderland, Krishna among the Cowgirls, King Kong, Rodin's *Kiss*, Dracula, Marilyn Monroe and modern stills of famous soldiers from their most violent battles. Over her bed was a life-size cut-out of himself on the edge of the cliff shouting "No!" when asked if Ettrick would surrender. His heart lurched — was Scottish Wat now a legend like the African Inongo, American Winesburg, Chinese Pingwu? — then he felt sick. After that shout he had stabbed a man who thought the battle over. It was a filthy way to enter the erotic fancies of a sixteen-year-old girl. However, he let her undress him and entered her bed.

Before nightfall he was amazed to find he liked Annie better than her mother. Though less experienced in love and coffee-making she had Nan's sensuality, humour and intelligence in a more slender and playful body. She made him feel powerful and wise. She also liked to

sleep with her ceiling clear as glass. He opened
his eyes early next morning and looked straight
up at a full moon between banks of hurrying
cloud. Not quite awake he felt Annie snuggle
warm at his side, her arm across his chest. He
thought he was lying with her on the floor of a
roofless cottage in a wilderness far to the north.
He seemed to remember escaping from a
shameful disaster which had befallen but at least
Annie and he were safe. Glad of this he fell
asleep again.

Later she wakened him by singing, *"A hero,
a hero, a hero in my bed, the first man to
fuck me is a heeeeero."*
Wat said, "You've fucked with others."
"Only with laddies. Lads don't count. Stop
interrupting and listen!
*A hero, a hero, a hero in my bed,
the first man to fuck me is a heeeeero.
I stole him from my mammy,
                    he wanted me instead,
O the first man to fuck me is a heeeeero."*
"Your mammy sent me here."
"Aye but it's good to pretend. Try it. You've
fought three wars, right?"
"Aye."
"And seven battles, right?"
"Aye. Your bloody uncle Jardine made the last

war continue for three."

"Seven bloody battles and never once wounded!" shouted Annie, "A miracle!"

Wat showed her his hands. She shouted, "Seven bloody battles and never once wounded by the *sworrrrrd*! UNSCATHED HERO JAGGED BY JEALOUS WHINBUSH AFTER GLORIOUS LAST-MINUTE MIRACLE-DRAW AGAINST OVERWHELMING ODDS! That's how the public eye should have announced it. If I was wee Wattie Dryhope," she said, kissing him sweetly, "I would pretend somebody was saving me for something gloriouser."

"Which somebody? Jesus MacGod or Accident MacDestiny?"

"MacGod of course. God orders you to conquer the universe for him but you say, 'No, sorry God, no till I've fathered a hundred lads on Annie Craig Douglas.' But I say, 'Go! I wilt never embrace thee nae mair until thou hast done God's will.' So you go conquering the universe till you're an old bald done dry withered wee man, and return to find me as sweet and sappy, young and perjink as ever. 'Nooky time!' you wheeze, 'Get them off.' 'Avaunt, Snotface!' I graciously retort, 'Or Wat or Julius Caesar or whatever you cry yourself. I cannae be thine, I am being shagged

continuous by a greater than thou.'
'Who?' croaks you. 'God,' says me, 'He sent
you conquering to get ye out of my short hairs
ha ha ha.' . . . Is something bothering you
Wattie?"

"Aye — your joke about me being kept for
something great. I once used to believe that,
Annie, but what great thing could it be?
Modern wars arenae great affairs. The only
greatness nowadays is in the folk building new
satellites and immortals creating new forms of
life."

She kissed his ear and whispered, "I'll tell you
a great thing you can do. This is my best time
of the month, you've been deep inside me, I'm
sure I've got my first bairn — what better new
thing can there be than that? And if it's a lad
promise you'll like him Wattie. And if he joins
the Ettrick warriors promise to be kind to him.
I've heard awful tales about how young laddies
get treated by older ones in the Warrior house."

"Don't believe all ye hear," said Wat, embracing
her, "The old soldiers keep an eye on things.
I'll protect him if I'm still about."

They were silent for a while. This was the
third day of their honeymoon. Wat feared Annie
would soon be bored and want to go and gossip
about him with her mother and sisters and

cousins. Wat was not bored. His queer dream
had given him an idea though he had been shy
of mentioning it till now. He said suddenly, "Do
you want your son to become a soldier, Annie,
and probably die before he's thirty? Or do you
want him to go to the stars and live till he
forgets you existed? Or would you rather he
joined the public eye and became a glib
commentator on other men's courage? Or left
the clean homes of Ettrick and lived dirty with
the gangrels?"

"It isnae a mother's business to want things
for her weans — it's the weans' business," said
Annie, puzzled, "Mothers who try to manage
their weans' lives always hurt them. Aunt
Mirren tried to stop her sons becoming soldiers
after Highlanders killed her first three at
Stirling Moss. She tried to make them starmen
by cramming them with physics and biology,
so they ran to the Warrior house as soon as
they could and came home hacked to pieces five
days ago. No wonder she's bitter. What are ye
trying to tell me Wat Dryhope?"

"I'm trying to tell ye about a new way of living
which hasnae been tried for centuries, Annie. I
want us to pretend there's nobody alive but
you and me . . ." (Annie sat up looking
interested) ". . . I want us to load a couple of
ponies with a tent, food, seeds, a cross-bow,

an axe and handy tools. I want us to ride far far to the north where the homes are few and the commons so mountainy that even gangrels seldom pass through. We'll find a broken old stone house, mibby a hunting-lodge built when there were no commons and the whole land was owned by a few plutocrats. We'll repair enough rooms to make a wee house of it. I'll get food by hunting and gardening, you'll cook it and make and mend our clothes."

"Go camping and play husband and wife?" cried Annie, smiling, "I played that game with my first laddie when I was twelve but only for a night. The alfresco shitting scunnered him in spite of the nooky — he called wiping his bum with dockens alfresco shitting. It'll be more fun with you."

"It wouldnae be just fun if you played it with me, Annie, it would be a way of life. I'd contrive a hygienic latrine and hot-water system. We wouldnae come back."

"But surely we would feel lonely after a few weeks!"

"Aye, very. We would hate it at first. Then the hard work of making an old-fashioned house together would teach us to depend on each other and love each other more than other men and women love each nowadays. Then the weans would come."

"Who would deliver them?"

"Me. I'm no stranger to blood and screams, Annie, I'll make sure nothing goes wrong."

"That's very cheery news, Wattie, but they'll be sad wee weans with only me to love — no aunties and grannies — no cousins to play with — no neighbours!"

"They'll have me as well as you."

"Bairns don't love dads."

"They would *have* to love me because they'd have nobody else — apart from you. I'd be always sleeping in the same house, bringing in the food you cook for us, teaching them how to hunt and plant and chop firewood and clean the latrine."

"But *no neighbours*, Wattie! The husbands and wives of historic times were so desperate for neighbours that they crowded into big huge ugly cities."

"Right!" said Wat, growing heated, "And the cities bred poverty, plagues and greedy governments! So a few brave men and women — pioneers they were called — left the cities for the wild in couples and made clean new lives there like we can make."

"Where and when did they do that?"

"In America three or four centuries ago."

"I'm sure they're no in America now. How long did they last?"

"I . . . I don't exactly know."

"Well, Wattie," said Annie in a friendly voice, "I'm sorry we've no plagues, poverty or governments to escape from, but I'll be your pioneer wife as long as you can bear it."

She shut her mouth tight to stop the smile at the corners becoming a grin. Wat saw it; she saw him see it, grinned openly and said, "But will wee me be able to content you when you've had big Rose of Cappercleuch and those Bowerhope twins and Lizzie of Altrieve and my mammy? Will you never want to see my mammy again? And have you forgot you'll grow old and die in that wilderness, Wattie? I thought men fought battles and became heroes because they were afraid to grow old."

He suddenly saw he had been a fool and the knowledge changed him. His face and neck reddened. With a sudden fixed smile, in a sing-song voice unlike his usual gruff one, he asked if she knew why he hated women. Annie, aghast, stared and trembled. He said, "I hate women for their damnable smug security and for always being older than me, always older and wiser! Even a kid like you, Annie Craig Douglas, has stripped me of my self-respect by knowing more about me than I know about myself. And when I'm dead you'll have lovers and babies and lovers and babies till you're a great-great-granny telling stories to wee girls. And I'll be one of your stories, the first warrior who fucked you — a daftie who wanted to run away and live alone with ye forever!"

Tears streamed from her eyes at this. She tried to embrace him. He pushed her away saying, "Keep your pity! I want the bad old days when wars had no rules and bombs fell on houses and men and women died together like REAL equals! Equal in agony and mutilation!"

"You're sick, Wattie. Your head's sick," said Annie, weeping, "You're worse than mad Jardine, your daddy."

His rage stopped at once.

"True!" he said, ruefully touching his brow, "And it's the only head I have. I'm sorry I lost my temper."

"As mad as his father," she muttered, pressing her hand to her womb, "O I'll have to ask about this."

She jumped out of bed and pulled on her dress. "Come back, Annie! Let's have another wee cuddle. I'm all right again. I said I was sorry."

"I don't want a mad baby, Wat."

"There is no such thing as a mad baby."

She slipped on her shoes without looking at him. Wat said, "Done with me, have you?"

"I'm too young to say, Wat. Bowerhope men

never come here now because twice Craig
Douglas women got weans with diseased blood
by Bowerhope — and the disease was curable.
I don't know if daftness is, and my mammy is
your dad's second cousin. The grannies will
know what's right. But O Wat," she wailed,
tears flowing down her cheeks again, "I liked
you fine before this! I *wanted* a bairn by you!"
He said, "Aye," and got up and started dressing.
She lingered by the door, drying her tears and
watching.

"I'll be in the Warrior house if your grannies
want to test my sanity," he said abruptly, "They
might want that before deciding you shouldnae
carry our bairn. But I'll no come back to Craig
Douglas unless invited — tell everyone that.
Tell Nan. Say goodbye to her for me. I never
much liked the Warrior house but now it seems
the one place where I'll be welcome — though
mibby no for much longer."

THREE

WARRIOR WORK

LIKE ALL WHO LOVED VISITORS
Annie had a room with a door onto the
veranda of her home, so Wat left Craig Douglas
that morning almost unnoticed at first. Near
the stables he heard musical jangling and shrill
shouts of, "Fall down you're dead!" — "No I
clonked you first!"

In a sandpit by the path a jumble of colourful
shelled creatures were hitting each other with
tiny swords: infants in helmets and armour
which pinged, twanged or clonked under
different strengths of blow. They stood still as
he drew level then the smallest ran to him and
stuttered breathlessly, "When I grow up I'll be
a Amazon and kill men like you do cousin
Wattie!"

She was a very wee girl. Wat paused and said

politely, "Name and age?"

"Betty. Four."

"Soldiers don't fight to kill each other, Betty. We fight to win the respect due to courage."

"Aye but killing men is still fun intit cousin Wattie?"

He shook his head hopelessly and entered the stable.

Three twelve-year-old lads knelt on the floor playing jorries. They sprang up, led the dapple grey from her stall, saddled and bridled her.

"Are you for the Warrior house Wat?" said one, "Can we come with ye?"

"I'm for a quiet ride on my lonesome lone, men," Wat told them sombrely, "I'm sorry your brothers got killed."

"But they helped us draw with Northumbria," said one gently as if offering consolation.

"Don't fool yourselves, men. Geneva will declare our draw a foul. I know because I was chief fouler. Open that door."

On the common he found his hands had healed enough to let him mount Sophia with dignity and after waving goodbye rode down to Yarrow. He suspected many eyes now watched him from the big house with the wood behind so did not look back. Wanting solitude he headed downstream toward Mountbenger along a

mossy track between tangled hedges which
followed the line of an old motorway.

The air felt close and heavy this morning
though little gusts of wind sometimes refreshed
it. A dull sky looked full of rain which never
fell. Yellow gorse on the hillside was the only
vivid colour. A mile above Mountbenger he
soaked his legs fording the river and rode up
the glen behind White Law, avoiding the houses
of Altrieve and Hartleap by keeping to the
hillside, and ascending Altrieve burn to the
saddle between Peat Law and the Wiss. Though
still brooding on the affection and respect he
might lose by his quarrel with Annie he was
soothed for a while by lonely distances which
grew more visible the higher he came. Houses,
cultivation, everything human was hidden in
dips between a wilderness of grey heights.
Vapour from powerplants was buried in ragged
cloud which dimmed the highest summits.
Nothing he now saw had changed since these
hills divided Scotland from England in the
historical epoch, the killing time when huge
governments had split the world into nations
warring for each other's property. He recalled
with pride that for centuries the border clans
had held aloof from England and Scotland,
siding with whichever nation was too weak to

tax them. But theft and murder had flourished in these rough hills too. The old ballads were full of it. The only wealth here had been small black cattle and when illness or famine thinned the herds the wife of a homestead set a plate with a pair of spurs on it before her man when he sat down to eat, a hint that he must now raid the English farms or starve. Yes, it was luxury to fear the ill opinion of the Ettrick aunts more than an empty belly, to worry about an unfair blow struck in a war between willing fighters, to suffer because he had frightened a healthy young girl in a moment of rage. He smiled and heard wind stir the grasses, near and distant cries of the whaups, and once what sounded like voices behind a clump of whins. Crossing a shoulder of hillside with a view into the gardens of Hartleap he saw what seemed half the family down there looking up at him. Later he glimpsed tiny figures withdraw behind the cairn on the summit of Bowerhope Law.

Signs of being watched and followed increased until he emerged from the woods above Thirlstane burn where the watchers and followers stopped trying to keep out of sight. He went down the gully with children of every age between eight and fifteen scrambling and leaping and dodging along the slopes on each side. The smallest rode ponies, two or three to a back. A surprising number were girls and the whole crowd was too big to be local — several must have come over from Eskdale or farther. Obviously something he did not know had made him interesting yet untouchable; only a huge, communal, fascinated shyness explained the movements of this company which covered the slopes beside him yet stayed out of talking range. His killing of the Northumbrian who held the standard had likely been condemned as a war crime so that Ettrick was now a shamed and beaten clan. Did these children hate or sympathize with him? They probably did not know themselves; they were waiting to learn how he would be received at the Warrior house. Wat feared nobody in the Warrior house, he dreaded nothing but the ill opinion of the women. Determined to learn the worst he sat upright and rode forward with a bold front unlike his usual brooding slouch.

A line of water as pale as the sky appeared above trees below; it was the head of Saint Mary's Loch and the Warrior house flag wagged against it. With various shouts the children raced downhill away from him and in less than five minutes he was alone again. If Sophia had not been a tired old pony he would have raced ahead of them; instead he paused, tempted by a track which ran sideways to Bowerhope where he was sure of a private welcome from a couple of sisters. Then a gleaming globe spun up from behind a blaeberry clump and hung before his face saying, "What is your reaction to the news from Geneva, Major Dryhope?"

He shut his eyes, clapped the pony's flanks with his heels and was carried straight downhill. He heard another voice, soft and female, say, "By all means treat the public eye with contempt Major Dryhope, but you must have something to say against Geneva's condemnation of your father and clan."

With an effort he kept his face immobile and eyes shut for at least three minutes. When he opened them the globe had vanished.

The Warrior house was built over the short river flowing into Saint Mary's Loch from Loch of the Lowes. Four steep glass-fronted gables, a central pyramidal skylight, a hexagonal tower faceted with mirrors made it look like a futuristic village in a 1930s Hollywood movie or a postmodern art gallery designed sixty years later. This archaic appearance was enhanced by an absence of powerplant. Wat saw that the plain before the eastern gable was covered by a

standing horde of children too young to be
cadets, and adolescents of both sexes, and older
men on horseback from houses normally
indifferent to warrior business. A greybeard and
three younger men from the musical house of
Henderland were conspicuous by the
instruments they held. The horsemen and pony
riders stood right and left of the path to the
entrance. As Sophia ambled down it Wat had a
dream-like sense of having done this before,
then remembered his walk from the stable
through the children of Craig Douglas. Passing
a group of boys with Annie in it he noticed
many of the Craig Douglas children were here
too. She was staring open-mouthed with hand
half raised as if wanting yet fearing to catch his
attention. He nodded absent-mindedly to her
for he was trying to understand the mood of
this dense crowd gazing at him with no obvious
sign of anger or pleasure. Then a shrill voice
from behind (and it sounded like Annie's) cried,
"Hooray for Wattie Dryhope!" and the whole
crowd began roaring, howling, yelling that too.
Through the roar he heard powerful drones
followed by vivid squeals. The Henderlands
were piping. Their tune swelled up and
overwhelmed the welter of cheering and it
was the tune of a song everyone had known
since childhood. In less than a minute the

crowd was singing —
"March, march, Ettrick and Teviotdale,
Why my lads dinna ye march
                              forward in order?
March, march, Eskdale and Liddesdale,
All the Blue Bonnets are over the Border!"
— so they liked him. Tears of relief streamed
down his face though he kept it rigid. He also
noticed, without pleasure, public eyes spinning
over the heads of the crowd. Recovering most
of the assurance he had lost since rolling off
the cliff he began to notice something
unpleasant in this unanimous bellowing of
what had once seemed a nostalgic old marching
song —
"Come from the hills
                      where your hirsels are grazing,
Come from the glen
                      of the buck and the roe;
Come to the crag where
                      the beacon is blazing,
Come with the buckler,
                      the lance and the bow!"
He reacted by scowling while Sophia, also
disliking the noise, broke into a clumsy little
gallop which brought him to the porch. Here
Boys' Brigade captains, one of them Wat's
twelve-year-old brother Sandy, swarmed round
him grinning like lunatics and jabbering

something in which *standard* was the only distinct word. He yelled, "Give Sophia a feed ye gowks — let Sandy get me a whisky," and leapt down and rushed inside.

Within the door he was stopped by a group of veterans: men over forty whose thick beards and moustaches did not hide their scars. Each shook his hand in turn, looking him straight in the eye and giving a firm little nod which struck him as more farcical than the communal roaring outside. Behind the veterans every cadet in Ettrick between eleven and fourteen years seemed crowded into the eastern lobby, grinning or open-mouthed or trying to look as grim as he felt himself. On the stair to the officers' mess the house servants stood like servants in the mansion of a Victorian duke assembled to welcome the young laird home. They were ranked behind the major domo, a stately giant with whiskers bushier than the fiercest veteran's. He said, "Master Wattie, I hope at last I may persuade you to a dram?" "Thanks Jenny. I have asked Sandy for one." "Master Sandy will receive it from my hands." The major domo led Wat upstairs processionally with Sandy beside him and the veterans in the rear. Martial discipline ensured a decent silence among them but did not lessen the deafening

bellow outside which still made sense to those who knew the words —
"England shall many a day
        tell of the bloody fray,
When the Blue Bonnets
        came over the Border!"

The officers' mess was under the gable above the eastern lobby. Wat was appalled by its emptiness. A week ago over two hundred cheerful men most of them in their late teens and twenties, had been drinking, laughing and chatting there; the dozen veterans now converging on the bar emphasized the difference. So did three cripples in orthopaedic chairs playing a game of whist: Colonel Tam Wardlaw, Rab Gillkeeket and Davie Deuchar. Wat had not seen them since the charge downhill with the standard. He went over and stood looking down on the game but they gave no sign of recognition though the Colonel said to the others, "Here comes trouble. I pass."
"Solo," said Rab.
"Misère," said Davie.
Wat covered his embarrassment by saying,

"Northumbria has made a bonny mess of you three."

"We might have been as fit as you if we'd rolled off a cliff," muttered Rab.

"True," said Wat abruptly, "Public eyeballs are snooping outside. D'ye mind doing with less daylight, Colonel?"

Colonel Wardlaw shrugged a shoulder.

"Frost the window, Jenny!" Wat called to the major domo behind the bar. Between the double sheets of glass a paperthin waterfall slid down then froze into starry white patterns which broke the appearance of the crowd and the hills outside into jagged shadows. Wat pulled a chair up to the table and sat watching the players until the Colonel said, "Do you want a hand?"

"I want news from Geneva."

Tam Wardlaw handed him a printed sheet. Wat held it without reading until his young brother put a whisky in the other hand.

"Wattie Dryhope is at The Macallan," sang Davie softly.

"Not possible!" said Rab, "Dryhope never touches alcohol. It upsets his chemistry."

"He's drinking it now," said the Colonel, "His chemistry must be out of order."

"Give us peace," muttered Wat and read the printout.

The Global and Interplanetary Council for War Regulation Sitting in Geneva has considered General Dodds's complaint against the recent draw between Ettrick and Northumbria United. General Dodds accuses Ettrick of obtaining the result by a foul pretence of surrender which did not take place, resulting in the murder of at least three Northumbrians who dropped their guard having been deceived into thinking the battle over. As proof of this he refers the Council to the public eye battle archive.

The Council has scrutinized the battle archive closely and believes there is good reason to condemn Ettrick but not for the action to which General Dodds objects. That a certain amount of deception is an inevitable and accepted part of combat is proved by that sword stroke known as a feint, nor is it unusual for hard-pressed troops to relinquish their standard to an enemy in order to counterattack more strongly. The Northumbrians holding the Ettrick standard believed the momentary pause signified surrender because they knew Ettrick could not win, being hopelessly outnumbered; but the Geneva Convention

*expressly states NO SOLDIER IS DEEMED
TO HAVE SURRENDERED BEFORE
HE DROPS HIS WEAPON OR OFFERS
THE HILT, BUTT OR HANDLE TO THE
OPPONENT. This did not happen. In the
slaughter following the resumption of
fighting after a twelve-second pause nearly
every Ettrick warrior died sword in hand.
If any dropped them or flung them away
General Dodds's troops did not notice.*

*But the Global and Interplanetary
Council for War Regulation Sitting in
Geneva is forced to condemn General
Jardine Craig Douglas for a war crime
worthy of the twentieth century. He was
wrong to lead his clan into a third day of
battle which must end in the death of nearly
all his men, many of them cadets recently
promoted from the Boys' Brigade. His own
death — however gladly embraced — is no
compensation for theirs, however gladly
they embraced it. The purpose of warfare is
not scoring points over an opponent: it is to
show human contempt of pain and
annihilation. Most armies do this without
exploiting the self-sacrificial urge of
trainees who admire their senior officers.
When such exploitation is proposed it is not*

*treachery for officers to defy the general who
proposes it. The Global and Interplanetary
Council for War Regulation Sitting in
Geneva regrets that Major Wat Dryhope was
the only Ettrick warrior who appeared to
recognize this fact . . .*

Wat chuckled and said loudly, "I've just read
the bit that explains why you chaps don't like
me now."

"Aye," said the Colonel, "You're suffering the
doom of everyone too good for their kindred."

"Wat Dryhope, humanity's darling," sang
Davie.

"Wattie! The standard!" whispered Sandy
urgently, "Ask them when we can —"

"Wheesht," said Wat and continued reading.

*For the past twenty years the Council has
noticed a tendency for small, competitive
clans to throw younger and younger cadets
into the battle line. True lovers of fighting
must deplore the harm this does to the noble
art of war. By his holocaust of young lives
General Jardine Craig Douglas has broken
the splendid line of Ettrick victories which
began with the century. At least a decade
must pass before Ettrick breeds and trains
enough adult soldiers to fight again at a
professional level.*

So the Global and Interplanetary Council for War Regulation Sitting in Geneva proposes three additions to the Geneva Convention.

1 - No war will extend to a third day of battle.

2 - No cadets of less than sixteen years shall be admitted to the battle line.

3 - When a standard leaves a field of battle by the interposition of a natural feature or phenomenon (cliff, crag, hill, cavern, canyon, pot-hole, volcanic vent or other geological formation; bog, swamp, shifting sands, stream, pond, river, lake, lagoon, sea, ocean or other body of water; breeze, wind, gale, tempest, sandstorm, hurricane, cyclone, tornado, lightning, fireball, aerolith or other meteorological event) the battle will be judged to have ended at that moment of the standard's departure from the field of battle, and victory will belong to the side which has lost fewest men.

The Global and Interplanetary Council for War Regulation Sitting in Geneva hereby declares a moratorium upon all armed conflict until a global and interplanetary referendum decides by a simple majority that each of these rules is

*accepted or rejected as part of the Geneva
Convention. Everyone over fifteen years of
age will be eligible to vote.*

*Meanwhile the Global Council for War
Regulation Sitting in Geneva declares that
these humanitarian proposals in no way
disparage the honesty and courage of the
Ettrick soldiers who carried out General
Jardine Craig Douglas's plan, while still
condemning absolutely their recklessness in
obeying him. The Global and Interplanetary
Council for War Regulation Sitting in
Geneva agrees with the public eye and the
mass of public opinion, in declaring the
battle between Northumbria and Ettrick a
draw; but also declare it a battle fought in
circumstances degrading to the senior
officers responsible, a kind of battle which
must never be repeated.*

Wat screwed the printout into a ball, cried,
"Good for Geneva!" and flung the ball lightly
at Colonel Wardlaw so that it bounced off his
ear. The Colonel flinched then muttered, "Hard
on your dad."
"It's right about the Dad! But we'll forgive his
bloody craziness if it gets three good rules like
that made law."

"You havenae drunk your whisky," said Rab.

"I don't need it now," said Wat, standing and going to them. They too were drinking Macallan. He tipped a neat third of his glass into each of theirs then signed to the barman for a strong coffee. It was brought.

"I hate Dryhope, he's a smug bastard," sang Davie softly.

"He cannae help it," said Rab, "He wins a world-famous draw by cheatery, fails in his suicide attempt and gets praised by Geneva for standing up to his daddy, though he did exactly what the old man telt him. Do you hate him too, Colonel?"

"Aye, but I hate his wee brother worse. Cadet Dryhope!" yelled the Colonel, "Stop standing there like a replica of Michel-fucking-angelo's David! In the days before the establishment of our democratic Utopia pretty wee soldiers who stood straight and cocky in front of crippled officers were given a hundred lashes. Slouch like your brother."

"But *the standard!*" whispered the boy trying to slouch and plead frantically at the same time.

"Clear out Sandy," said Wat. Sandy left. As he opened and shut the door they heard a burst of hubbub from below pierced by the music of pipes playing a coronach.

"Colonel Wardlaw!" said Wat sharply, "Tell me

now why grown men like the Henderlands and Foulshiels — men with no interest in warrior business — are waiting downstairs among a crowd of weans and lassies."

"I don't know," muttered Wardlaw.

"Will I go down and find out?" asked Wat.

"The game's a bogie, men," said the colonel to the other players. He flung his cards on the table and turned his chair to face Wat. Davie dealt the cards again and went on playing with Rab.

In a low voice pitched for Wat's ears only Colonel Wardlaw said, "Look at my face, Dryhope."

Wat did so with frank pleasure because it took his attention away from the surgical corset holding the Colonel's body together; then he saw that only a pale-blue left eye showed intelligence. The bloodshot right stared fixedly sideways from a pupil so big it blotted out the iris.

"Sorry, Tam," said Wat quietly, "I thought only your lower parts were hurt."

"No. The head has the worst damage and not where you see it. There's a sore buzzing inside

that I try to think isnae an insect. I wish you'd
spent a month wandering the hills, Wattie,
because I need peace. I said *Here comes
trouble* when you arrived because you make
us a quorum — the three officers and one
colonel needed to dispatch urgent regimental
business. Wattie, neither me nor Rab nor Davie
could dispatch a paper aeroplane. We're as queer
and gruesome as a week with nine Mondays.
I'm done with soldiering, Wattie. We're all done
with soldiering. The knocks we got from
Northumbria are mainly why but that message
from Geneva finished us. A spate of others
marked *urgent* followed it. They're in this
pouch —" (Tam clapped a satchel under the
armrest of his chair) "— I darena look at them."
"Gie's them," said Wat, stretching out a hand,
"Jenny could have answered them but I'll do it
faster. I bet half can be ignored and the rest
answered with *Thanks for your friendly letter*.
And forget Geneva, Tam. It said the truth, but
no honest soldier or kind woman will scorn us
for obeying our elected commander."

Wat put the wad of sheets on a nearby table
and quickly sorted it into two piles, one of blue
sheets from public eye companies, one of pink
sheets meaning warrior business. Tam watched
with an expression in which weariness,

indifference and anxiety oddly blended. Two minutes later Wat lifted the blue pile and said, "These are from every big eye company there is, the nearest in the Lothians, the farthest in the satellite belt. We know they want to exploit public excitement about a battle which for us is past and done, so we answer them this way." With a sharp wrench Wat tore that pile in two, laid the bits on a chair then sorted through the other, this time glancing at a line or two before laying each one aside. Once he paused and said, "Colonel Tam, why were our wee lads yattering about standards?"

"They want permission to fish our old pole out of the North Sea. They're feart some of Dodds's tykes will get it first and melt it intae the roots of a Northumbrian powerplant."

Tam sipped his whisky. Wat finished reading then turned and said, "Cellini's Cosmopolitan Cloud Circus remind you that tomorrow night they will pay homage to mankind's most famous draw with a completely new spectacle called From the Big Bang to the Battle of the Ettrick Standard: a Creative Evolutionary Opera to be performed on the hills round Selkirk. The rest are congratulations from clan chiefs everywhere, some of them world champions. Many blame Geneva for what some call *a nursemaid attitude to the noble art of*

war. And here's one to cheer you — Shafto of
Northumbria wishes us well and says he didn't
subscribe to Dodds's protest against the draw.
This other is the only one needing a careful
answer. Border United — the chiefs of Eskdale,
Teviotdale, Liddesdale and the Merse — regret
our loss of folk fit to train the next generation
of Ettrick fighters. They will lend us officers
of their own, on a rotation basis, not to fight
battles of course but to get our youngsters
ready for them. What do you say to that?"

"Answer it yourself. Answer it how you like,"
said Tam, "I telt the truth when I said I'm done
with every game but cards."

His haunted expression did not change but
something like a smile twisted it. In a hollow,
resounding voice which all in the mess turned
to hear he announced: "As Colonel of the
Ettrick Army met in a quorum of my fellow
officers in the absence of our dearly deceased
General Jardine Craig Douglas, I appoint YOU,
Major Dryhope, my successor with full plenary
powers to do what the hell you like until such
time as you get yourself — or someone else —
elected general in Jardine's stead. Arise Colonel
Dryhope, greatest of Ettrick's sons! I also
declare that I and Rab Gillkeeket and Davie
Deuchar are henceforth a trio of clapped-out
veterans fit for nothing but games our grannies

taught us. Deal me a hand, lads."
He turned his chair back to the card table where
Davie Deuchar, after slowly clapping his hands
together twice, shuffled and dealt.

Wat had risen to his feet when the Colonel
told him to. He now stood wondering why
his new appointment did not surprise him,
though he had certainly never expected it. The
obvious answer was that only he was fit for it.
He wished Colonel Wardlaw had passed on the
job in kinder language. The veterans at the bar
saluted him then raised and drained their
glasses. He saluted back and was wondering
what to do next when the major domo
approached, bowed, murmured that the crowd
downstairs had been long awaiting an
announcement, and asked if Colonel Dryhope
wished the decision the quorum had just
expressed through Colonel Wardlaw to be made
public.
"Verbatim?" said Wat, sharply.
"No sir: in a form suitably edited for the public
ear," said Jenny as reproachfully as if his
intelligence had been questioned.
"Go ahead Jenny."
Jenny left by a door behind the bar and Wat
stood listening intently. He heard throbbings
of a speaker then a swelling cheer which got

louder until even here it was uncomfortably loud. It did not stop. Wat wondered why there was something soothing in the sound.

"Shut them up Dryhope!" yelled Tam, "Talk to them! The glaikit sumphs want their new sweetheart to simper audibly."

Jenny approached again, bowed, put his moustache ticklingly close to Wat's right ear and said, "Does Colonel Dryhope wish to respond to the ovation by loudspeaker, or will he prefer to personally address the Boys' Brigade in the hall of the standards? In either case his words will be relayed to the crowd outside."

Wat felt the moustache withdraw and saw Jenny's large flat ear presented to his mouth. He said thoughtfully, "Tell them that in fifteen minutes I'll speak from the roof of the eastern porch — that will give the Boys' Brigade time to go outside. But first tell their captains to come here to the mess. And . . . and I must make a private call to Northumbria first. The speech will start in thirty minutes, not fifteen." He went out with Jenny and the cheering stopped soon after.

Later he returned, spoke briefly with veterans at the bar, went to the door, admitted six Boys' Brigade captains and talked to them while Jenny served them half pints of shandy. This was their first time in the officers' mess and they behaved with fitting dignity. Then Wat approached Tam, Rab and Davie and said quietly, "One last request, lads."

"Request refused," said Wardlaw, "What is it?"

"I'm making a speech from the porch roof and want you with me."

"Ye want us for a *balcony* appearance, Colonel Dryhope?" sang Davie loudly, "Like the clique who stood about behind Hitler above the Potsdamstrasse? Or made Stalin look less lonely outside the Kremlin? An hour ago you frosted that window to shut out public eyeballs. I knew power corrupts but didnae know it corrupted *that* fast!"

"You don't need our support, Dryhope," said Tam Wardlaw sourly.

"O I do, I need all three of you," said Wat, kneeling so that his face was level with theirs, "Our families want to be proud of Ettrick, no matter what Geneva says. That's why folk of every sort except aunts and grannies are waiting outside. We can make them proud if we stand together. I'll be out there with old Megget and Cappercleuch and Hartleap, veterans who fought at Ilkley and Kettering and Sunningdale. I'll have captains of the Boys' Brigade beside me, champions of the future. How can I inspire pride when the best soldiers to survive our hardest fight — three of the quorum who made me Colonel — sit girning in the shadows like sulky bairns while the rest of us stand in the sunlight trying to look brave? Ye dour lazy bitches, ye don't even need to stand! You've nae legs! All ye need do is roll your chairs through the door ahint ye."

"Does he *persuade*, Deuchar?" wondered Rab Gillkeeket, "If my glands were not disjaskit his rhetoric would get the adrenalin flowing, but does he *persuade*?"

"He appealed to our clan patriotism," pondered Davie, "Then flattered, shamed and mocked. This blend of the pawkie, couthie and earthy was once thought characteristic of the Scottish peasantry but Wat isnae a peasant and we're naething but wrecks. What says Wardlaw?"

Tam Wardlaw said violently, "We'll do it and be done with it."

Wat nodded, told them to be ready in five minutes then went to a table where Jenny had laid a tumbler of milk and plate of sandwiches, his first meal that day.

The starry film of frost vaporized and drifted up leaving the wall transparent. A section of it opened onto a roof garden over the porch. Wat sent the veterans and boys' captains out with drinks in their hands to sit where they liked, then he and the cripples followed, wending through the tables to the rail that served as parapet. He put a chair between Wardlaw and Deuchar and sat with arms folded on the rail, waiting.

This informal arrival drew little attention. The cloud had broken letting afternoon sunlight through. The crowd, much bigger than when he arrived, was now in a holiday mood. Picnic parties sat chatting on the turf; groups surrounded fiddlers, wrestlers, singers, debaters. The kind of alcohol and snuff no housemother would synthesize was being traded by gangrels in return for wristcoms and items of clothing. Some people in bright outlandish garb were advertising the cloud circus. He noticed a woman on twenty-foot-tall stilts covered by red and white striped trousers. She wore a star-spangled top hat and tail coat, and stepped about over the heads of the crowd waving in a comically threatening way a parasol shaped like a nuclear bomb cloud. Children on the verge of the crowd raced ponies through bracken and heather. The only solemn touches were groups of horsemen who had been waiting since morning, some mounted, some standing at their animals' heads. One thing that worried him was a public eye a yard from his face. No open-air meeting as big as this had met in peacetime for a century so public eyes would intercut his speech with film of leaders haranguing huge crowds in the late historical era. Since he and his comrades were not standing in formal groups he would look, as well as sound, very different. He glanced at the tiny microphone on his chest and decided to speak seated, with folded arms.

Suddenly he noticed part of the crowd he had overlooked. On the ground before the porch the Boys' Brigade stood in six straight ranks. Feet apart, arms clasped behind them, faces tilted up toward Wat, the exact stance of each one made him a childish replica of the rest. Captainless, ordered outside by a servant to hear the new colonel's speech, they had chosen this way to show the discipline that divided them from civilians. Wat stood up, smiling, and bent toward them. He muffled the microphone with one hand, saluted with the other and called down, "Break ranks, men, this —"
He had been going to say *is not a military occasion* but a huge hollow woofing drowned

his words: the microphone was more sensitive than he had known. He stood erect and saw everyone was now attending; the only sound was the fading drone of a bagpipe and the rustle of folk turning or standing to see him more clearly. He said quietly, "This is Wat Dryhope about to speak to friends. Will the public eye please shift from between us?"

The eye moved slightly aside. His voice had carried to the back of the crowd without manic-sounding reverberations but he sensed an immediate excitement, a hunger for the emotional unity that had greeted his descent from the hillside. This excitement gave him a feeling of righteous power because, unlike dark-age politicians, he was going to dissolve that mindless unity by the calm delivery of sensible information. He said, "I havenae much to say but most of you have been waiting here for hours so I'll sit here and say it. If you've any sense you'll follow my example — that's a suggestion. The junior cadets will meanwhile break ranks and sit on the ground — that's an order."

He sat down with arms folded on the railing. The Boys' Brigade did as he commanded. With a murmur suggesting amusement all but the horsemen followed their example. Wat gave his speech.

"I suppose you've come here to learn things you might not get from the public eye, which exists to make entertainment out of serious war games. Here are the straight facts. Colonel Tam Wardlaw here has given me his job because I'm the only soldier in Ettrick with two arms, two legs and no internal injuries. I am in this healthy state because General Craig Douglas ordered me to lead the vanguard, which was the safest job in our last battle. Our whole army was organized to get me safe to the cliff top where I did my wee trick with the standard. While getting me there our army was almost wholly destroyed but I'm all right. No wonder Geneva condemned that tactic.

"My present health is also due to me rolling off the cliff when the massacre started, and to a bush that caught me after I'd done that, and to General Shafto of Northumbria who pulled me off it. Less than an hour ago I spoke to General Shafto and told him we feared that North Sea currents might wash our old pole out of reach. He is sending divers from Whitby to locate it and attach a buoy. Tomorrow we can recover it when we like. Good men, the Northumbrians.

"What of the future? As Geneva says, ten

years must pass before we can breed and train another professional army so there is no urgent need to elect a new general. Our wounded officers will recover, though we cannot say how completely. Some of our veterans may return to active service. In three or four years young captains beside me here will be old enough to fight. There are potential generals on this platform, and standing among you, and many more at home with their aunts. Building an army comes before choosing a general. Luckily our neighbours on the banks of Tweed and Leader, Teviot and Esk will lend officers to train youngsters and new recruits."

He stood up and said, "That was my news. Goodbye."

He saluted and was turning to leave when a voice said, "Can I say a word to you Colonel Dryhope?"

It was a firm voice, quiet, adult, male and it came from the crowd.

"You've said several already," said Wat turning back, "Seven at least. How did you say them through the Warrior house speakers?"

"I'm Archie Crook Cot," said the voice. This caused a burst of laughter; the Crook Cots were famous for their electronic expertise.

"That explains it," said Wat, looking amiably

toward a group of horsemen with one stout rider a little before the rest, "What have you to say, Archie?"

"Just that Geneva's wrong about the ten years. More than two hundred full-grown Ettrick men are here to sign on as recruits today and you may get as many tomorrow. Our average age is eighteen or so. If we put our backs into the training . . . and we will lads, won't we?" he asked turning in his saddle — there was a widespread shout of "*Aye!*" — "Then you'll have a full adult fighting force in less than a year."

The last words were drowned in a storm of cheering as the whole crowd of younger folk jumped to their feet shouting and clapping and laughing. The Henderlands raised their pipes, puffed their cheeks and were obviously about to raise the sound level.

"*YE GOWK ARCHIE!*" yelled Wat, "*YE DOITED GOMERIL! YE STUPIT NYAFF! YE BLIRT!*"

The amplification was so great that the crowd was silenced, many clapped their hands to their ears, Tam Wardlaw turned his chair and sped back to the mess. With an effort Wat said more quietly, "Men become soldiers, Archie Crook Cot, because we're no good at anything else! The Crook Cots are teachers, wizards, gurus in the mandarin network! When I was in the satellite belt people who heard my voice said, 'You're Scottish. Which part?' 'Ettrick,' said I. 'Ettrick?' said they, 'Do you know the Crook Cots?' and because I had played with ye when we were bairns their respect for me doubled. Whenever crazy chemicals provoke a new virus — or maybe it's the other way round, I'm too ignorant to ken — the star seeders want the problem keyed into a mandarin web with at least one Crook Cot guru in it. Why should anyone with an ounce of intellectual talent train for a life of grievous bodily harm?"

"You think we havenae the spunk for it Wat?" jeered a voice from somewhere and provoked scattered laughter.

"Wattie," said Archie pleasantly, "There's no use saying what our aunties told us this morning. You're a great soldier and have no illusions about fighting. I'm a guru and don't think much of my job either. I enjoy playing mandarin on keyboards, spinning threads in a web of knowledge that will join the stars one day, but I'm no immortal genius. Immortals talk to me like an equal because I know their language and they find me useful, but when my cousin Willie told me yesterday he was off to join the army I discovered I was an Ettrick patriot before anything else."

"*WHY?*" said Wat sharply enough to quell the

beginnings of another cheer.

"For fun," said Archie and across the sea of heads Wat saw a toothy grin divide the round face of the squat figure on the horse, "I enjoyed spreading consternation through an eternal network which thought me a dependable unit. I like the amazement, admiration and grief my sisters, aunts and grannies now feel for me. But I most like astonishing myself. What! Will a guru like me drill for months in the martial arts and sleep in his cloak during forced marches over the hills? The notion is too fantastic to be resisted. Mibby I'll crack under the strain. I doubt it. We'll see."

The cheer which now arose was too loud to be quelled. Wat strolled up and down the platform waiting for it to fade. He noticed that the veterans and Boys' Brigade captains now stood behind him in the formal groups he had meant to avoid, but now they would have looked silly seated so he gave them an approving nod. The more he thought about this renewal of the army the more exciting it seemed. When he again faced the crowd a small tight smile twisted his mouth. He silenced the fading din with a gesture and said, "There is no law to stop any man in Ettrick joining us if he's healthy and crazy enough to do it. If I tried

to keep ye out now you'd think I wanted all
the wee boys to myself. Go back to your homes
and send your names and physical profiles here.
If you're fit you'll get word saying what to bring
for your first term of training which, I promise,
will be no picnic. You've seven days to change
your minds while I work out a completely new
training programme. Goodbye."

He turned his back on a new wave of
cheering and went quickly into the mess where
a fit of huge yawning seized him.
"You need a rest, Colonel Dryhope," murmured
Jenny.
"Rest and privacy, Jenny."
"The commander's quarters are ready for you
sir," said Jenny and led him from the mess into
the communications room, led him from
there by lift to an apartment he was visiting
for the first time. The last man to use it
had been his father.

FOUR

PUDDOCK PLOT

WAT WAKENED sitting on a lavatory pan, sure he had not been unconscious for more than a minute or two. On leaving the cubicle he could not at first remember where he was and why. Through clear walls on every side he saw hills, woods, lochs he had known from childhood. They were lit by familiar evening sunlight but in an order he could not recognize. A central part was missing — the Warrior house. Then he realized he was above it. The Ettrick commander's apartment was in a tower which from outside he had always thought a solar heating duct. Delighted by his new elevation he let out a bark of laughter which almost hurt his throat. Without hurry he bathed then dressed in a clean suit of loose clothes which fitted perfectly. He walked about glorying in the soft carpet, the spare efficient furniture, the combination of perfect comfort with a view commanding the countryside he loved best. No wonder his father had preferred this place to houses where all apartments were on the same level.

"Privacy and power," he murmured aloud, "Power and privacy."

He would hate leaving here if someone else became general, but who else could they make general? Three days ago he had honestly meant to nominate Joe for the job but then a new army had seemed years away. If Archie Crook Cot was right Ettrick would perhaps be able to fight again in six months. Some recruits would certainly crack under their training — he hoped so, it would show the strength of the rest — but only Wat Dryhope would be fit for the general's job if he did not waste time daydreaming. Sitting at a keyboard Colonel Dryhope summoned a series of training programmes and started adapting them to the probable needs of middle-aged recruits.

There was a slight cough and he saw Jenny laying a meal on a table.

"Yes, it's time I ate," said Wat, "And I appreciate your quality of silence. But next time warn me before you enter. A quiet tinkle will do. When a chain of thoughts is being connected even wee surprises can break it."

"I will do so in future, Colonel Dryhope, but may I speak?"

"Fire away," said Wat, sitting at the table and uncovering a dish of roast woodcocks.

"I have served four Ettrick commanders, Colonel Dryhope, and those who worked hardest kenned how to relax. Three relaxed with alcohol but you, I think, are your father's son?"

"Aye?"

"Messages await your attention, Colonel Dryhope. Some will be invitations," said Jenny, pointing to a shelf where a stack of papers lay under a wallprinter.

"Sort them for me," said Wat pouring gravy on small brown bodies, "Put messages about warrior business on my desk. Put messages from public eye channels down the waste chute. Bring the rest here."

For several minutes Wat sucked delicate meat from small bones and disposed of a salad. He was pouring coffee when Jenny laid a sheaf of pale violet papers beside the cup. Wat said, "Good man, Jenny. Have my pony saddled and waiting in twenty minutes. I may go out."

"Would not a horse be a more suitable mount, Colonel Dryhope? The late general's favourite, Bucephalus, is both elegant and docile."

"I'm no an elegant horseman," said Wat
pleasantly, "Go away and do what I said, Jenny."

The prints contained intimate portraits and
were mostly from women who adored him for
qualities they had noticed through the public
eye. A few were from older women he knew
well; they pleased him best. He was hurt to
find nothing from Nan but she hated warrior
business and probably disliked him being a
colonel. A note from her daughter Annie
begged him to call at once. He did. In a voice
full of happiness and tears she said, "O Wattie
Wattie. O Wattie Wattie."
"Hello there."
"O Wattie I was *daft* to be feart when ye were
mad at me this morning, my aunties and
grannies have *telt* me I was daft, all soldiers
have wee mad fits when they've been in bad
wars, they say, and it doesnae hurt the bairns
they get so I can see ye again, Wattie! Tonight
if ye like!"
He took a moment to remember what she was
raving about then said awkwardly, "That's
good, Annie, but tonight I want to see your
mother, if she'll have me. Do you think Nan
will have me?"
He heard a wailing from Craig Douglas which
made him glad he had not made a visual

connection. He said hastily, "Yes Annie. Fine.
Aye. Mhm. Since your grannies don't mind I'll
mibby see ye in a fortnight, but of course —"
(he tried to cheer her with a joke) "— your mammy
might want to give me to one of your sisters."
She cut him off.

He sighed and looked out. The clear sky was
now patterned with clusters of saucerlike
cloudlets, the remotest tinted pink by the
evening sun. Beneath each was a house, in each
house was at least one bedroom where he would
be ecstatically welcome. He regretted leaving
his work on the training programme but Jenny
was right, he would work better if he relaxed
first. He stared at a cloudlet beyond the
wooded top of Bowerhope Law. Beneath was
Bowerhope house, less than two miles away by
the shore path. Two friendly sisters there had
been kind to him more than once. Their private
names were Myoo and Myow and they always
bedded together. He called their room at
Bowerhope and said, "Myow?"
"Myoo."
"Colonel Wat Cat is coming, pussies."
"Mwoopee."

When he reached the path to Bowerhope
shadows were darkening under the trees but

there was a soft glow in the sky and on the loch. The path was level and without abrupt turnings. Sophia, refreshed by rest and good feeding at the Warrior house, went at a satisfying pace. Wat, happy in his destination, gave himself to more thought about the training programme.

Men usually became soldiers through a disciplined extension of war games they had played as children, but many of the world's best fighters, like himself, had come late to the army after work with other things, perhaps because delay had strengthened their determination. He would soon command the first determined army of late starters the world had seen since Cromwell's in the historical era. Then he remembered George Washington's troops — Napoleon's generals — Ulysses S. Grant — Leon Trotsky — Che Guevara. The world would be watching him with these in mind, a wonderful, fearful thought! He prevented excitement by thinking how to work harder and set better examples than the trainee officers lent by neighbouring clans, though these would all be good men. He thought of Archie Crook Cot, a famous physicist, intelligent man, very good speaker. His muscular strength and co-ordination were better than his bulky body suggested. Like many gurus he relaxed by hunting and fishing and had gained local fame by it. Archie would adapt fast to war games and must already be imagining himself general of Ettrick. Wat smiled and muttered, "No yet Archie. Let's see you after your first wee war." He would manage Archie by giving him tough assignments and, if he handled them well, by promoting him. He would ask him, even now, to pick a company of volunteer divers and bring the Ettrick standard back from the North Sea. This would show Colonel Dryhope in command from his first day in office, and delight Ettrick traditionalists, and soothe Crook Cot's vanity. Wat raised his wristcom to call Archie and saw the dial was lightless except for the word BEAMBLOCKED. He shook and tapped it, wondering why it gave such an impossible reason for malfunction. Beams were directed from satellites by human agencies. In a squabble between two satellites for a habitat zone a mischief maker had once temporarily blocked a rival's part of network, the nearest thing to lawless fighting humanity had known for over a century, but nobody, however mischievous, used interplanetary energies to play a prank on someone's wrist communicator.

Suddenly his ear was teased by the repetition of a sound no louder than the lapping of small waves on the shore to his left: an occasional soft tinkle from the wooded slope on his right. Looking there he saw a glowing violet spot travelling against darkness under the branches: obviously (he thought) an oddly coloured public eye many yards away. With another soft tinkle it floated out in front of his face. It was a bubble less than half an inch across with a violet outline and contained a head with abundant black shoulder-length hair and a womanly face, though too small to be recognized. He stared sternly at a point above it and heard a tiny, distinct very girlish English voice which became tough American then huskily Germanic. Throughout these accent shifts it remained mockingly, whorishly female and roused him in a way he detested.
"Please don't ignore me sir, I am the fairy Tinker Bell who will make all your dreams come true, but you can call me Phyllis Marlowe. I'm a private eye, not a public eye and I'm absolutely and utterly yours, darlink."
"Fuck off," said Wat coldly, "I'm giving no

interviews to crack-brained voyeurs, public or private."

The bubble recoiled as if struck and settled on Sophia's head between the ears. These twitched as the small voice shrilled, "Ooooooo why are you so croooooooel to me?" and made sounds like bitter sobbing. Sophia did not alter her pace. Wat urged her into a jolting trot which was the fastest she could go but the bubble stayed between her ears.

"I'll tell you a story, dearie," said a voice amazingly like a Scottish granny's, "There was once a wee lad who didnae like the lassies of Ettrick and ordinary war games, he liked wild historical wars that were fought without rules and changed the world, wars fought with wild glamorous women and explosions and spaceships which carried him to new worlds. In sentimental moments he also enjoyed gardening, so he decided to be a star seeder."

"A third of humanity starts that way," said Wat scornfully.

"This boy was unique, dearie. He was taller than the rest and ashamed of it because he thought women couldnae like him — and he certainly didnae want any poor lassie who did. That's why he wanted new worlds, worlds where he would not be an outsider because he dominated them. He also had the smeddum to work hard at what he hated, so he must have been terribly unhappy. After three painful years of keyboard work he knew enough astrophysics and biology to get into space, though his mind was not exactly scientific. Two years in satellite greenhouses ended his love of gardening. A talk with an immortal ended his dream of reaching new worlds — he could only do that by forgetting childhood dreams. He came home, became a soldier like his daddy and is now a world-famous hero. That won't content him."

"Tell me what I don't know."

"Oui, at our next meeting, chéri," the voice whispered with a French accent, "The meeting where we become love-*ers*."

Wat laughed. He seldom noticed comic situations but this seemed one. He looked at the bubble in a friendly way. It now contained a mouth with full lips precisely crimsoned in a 1940s Hollywood fashion which had been revived at least thrice a century since. He said, "As you're synthesized from the soundtracks of ancient movies I won't get much joy from *that* meeting. You're probably not even a woman. Real women don't use satellite technology to seduce a man."

There was a pause in which he let Sophia resume the pace she found easiest. The voice

said, "An intelligent deduction, Colonel
Dryhope, but I am very much a woman. This
sophisticated foreplay ensures we will meet in
the body without inhibitions, but it is *your
soul* I want to seduce."

The voice now sounded like a soft-speaking
south-east English woman with a slight exotic
flavour of Caribbean or southern U.S.A. Wat
had heard it before. He said amiably, "Why do
you want that?"

A man's voice spoke. It took Wat a few seconds
to recognize his own.

"Give me a period of excitement when folk
thought they were making a better world . . .
Rage, not sorrow is my disease . . . I hate
women for their damnable smug security . . . I
want the bad old days when wars had no rules
and bombs fell on houses and men and women
died together like REAL equals! Equal in their
agony and mutilation! . . . Privacy and power,
power and privacy."

Wat felt pressure in his heart and eardrums. He
breathed carefully to prevent useless rage. He
pretended to yawn then said that using satellite
technology to invade private lives was the sort
of criminal intrusion the world had outgrown
over a century ago, was against the Geneva
Convention, was infantile bad manners.

"Yeah, but I'm a real wild child and an

outlaw, honey," said the voice Americanly, "I'm a professional hooker who has *hooked you*."

"You're also a media person. You spoke to me in your English voice from a public eye ball this morning, one that jumped out of a blaeberry bush when I came down by Thirlstane. How can you be public and private too?"

"How can you be Colonel Dryhope in Ettrick Warrior house and your aunties' Wattie at home? Media people also get into more than one set, Colonel Dryhope. The more sets we belong to the more power we hold. I'm in more than a dozen and am now forming the most powerful set in the world. It has two members — you and me."

"I'll discuss this chat with Archie Crook Cot," said Wat grimly, "You may have heard of him. I don't think he'll need more than an hour of networking to find the beam you're using, and where you are, and who you are."

For a while the lips stayed slightly parted. Their owner was either thinking hard or listening to instructions from someone else, but Wat did not feel outnumbered.

"I would feel very hurt if you told Archie Crook Cot about me, Colonel Dryhope," said the mouth at last, "Others would suffer too. You are not a man who can be frightened, but your clan might suffer most."

"I'm no feart of mysterious threats," said Wat grinning, "Nor feart of people who repeat things I said idly or in a bad temper. Why not replay what I said before the battle when I spoke to save the Ettrick weans? Geneva noticed that."

"That is not the side of you which attracts me," said the mouth softly, "Do you not know that many women desire to feel themselves helpless in the arms of a powerful man they identify with God?"

"If you're a masochist in search of a violent brute find another soldier. The breed is not extinct."

"Ah, but you are so *wrong*, chéri! The breed is practically extinct. Other soldiers waste their violence in conventional war games then go home to be nursed by their conventional aunts and sweethearts. And I am more than a sensual body — I too am an outsider who cannot bear this world governed by aunts and grannies. It has lasted too long, it is stale, it needs renewal. You feel this too, Wat — that is why you wanted to start a reich of two with Annie Craig Douglas. It would have been too small for you. Renew the world with me! It will be dangerous work but neither of us fear danger. It will also need political intelligence."

"Rhetoric!" said Wat impatiently, "If you've a concrete proposal, Ms. Media, propose it in sensible modern language. The adjective *political* became meaningless a century and a half ago."

"If you stay silent about this meeting . . ." said the mouth slowly, ". . . I will propose to you tomorrow."

"When?"

"When you return to the Warrior house. Promise to be silent till then."

"I promise nothing. I won't speak of this till we've met. Let that content you."

The bubble swooped to his right ear and whispered, "Have you ever fucked a media bitch or do you only do it to pussies?"

"Neither bitches nor bubbles."

"If you gossip about this we will never meet *in the flesh*, chéri. You will also lose the chance to recreate the world in the image of your wildest dreams — and quickly! Bonsoir. I will now vanish with a most melodious twang but remember, I hear every word you say and love most the words you fear to say. Our love-making will be different than with others. It will strengthen, not relax you. I will teach you not to be ashamed."

He turned in time to see the bubble vanish with a melodious twang.

It was now after sunset but a silvery scatter of pebbles showed the path. The digits on his wristcom were glowing again. He dialled Archie Crook Cot and asked if he would organize the retrieval of the standard, taking the veteran General Megget and three Boys' Brigade captains with him to show it was an Ettrick Warrior business. Archie Crook Cot, sounding pleased, said yes, he had been worrying about the standard. He would also take Jimsy Henderland (an excellent diver) and start early. Wat told him to use the Warrior house sky sledges but contact General Shafto first, then hesitated and said, "Report to me at once when you return."

He switched off, wondering if he would regret not having given Archie a more technical job right away. Soon after he saw the lights of Bowerhope. He was enthusiastically welcomed but it was not a satisfying visit. Myoo said, "Getting colonelized has weakened you, Wat Dryhope. You don't seem with us."

Our dreams review events of the waking day, working them into the pattern of early memories and wishes which is our character. Wat dreamed easily about his squabble with Annie because he expected young girls to be bothersome. His triumphal arrival at the Warrior house and swift promotion to commander also fitted his dreams; he had not expected it but early efforts had prepared him for it. Nothing had prepared him for the conversation on the path to Bowerhope. His dreams turned nasty and woke him long before dawn. He lay perfectly still, unwilling to rouse the friendly bodies he lay between, unable to rest for troublesome thoughts.

He thought first about people in public eye companies. Broadcasters of war games clearly enjoyed getting close to bloodshed without being hurt. A woman of that sort with a taste for tall graceless carnaptious soldiers could easily use public equipment to contrive private meetings with them. But Wat's movements had been followed, his words recorded and edited for at least five days before a blocking beam had isolated him from the intelligence network. Through a unique device he had been told that *here and now between Myoo and Myow* he was still being surveyed. No single person could use so much energy for a private purpose without being noticed as a selfish waster and interrupted. Since the media bitch did not fear interruption she must be part of a team making a programme about him. This broke the first rule in the bill of human rights: NOBODY WILL BE USED BY ANOTHER WITHOUT KNOWING AND WILLING IT. But a team breaking this rule must be working in secret, and secret societies (like governments, stock exchanges, banks, national armies, police forces, advertising agencies and other groups who made nothing people needed) had ended with the historical era. The modern intelligence net was open to everyone. It could only be used secretly by people arousing no curiosity, yet the media bitch had deliberately aroused his. What could such people want that they could not get openly? The earliest Christian churches, the Freemasons and Trade Unions had been secret societies. They believed all good people were equal in the eyes of God or natural justice, so unjust governments had banned them. Big governments later created their own secret societies, the F.B.I., C.I.A., K.G.B.D., M.I.5 which lied and tortured, robbed and killed in ways their employers could publicly deny. And people had been robbed and killed by Al Capone's mob, the Mafia and the I.R.A. which were also secret forms of government. Wat's head ached with efforts to imagine reasons for

secrecy on an earth whose largest government
was the family and where each family had what
it needed.

After a few seconds he left the bed by
creeping carefully to the foot. By the glowing
calendar on a screen he saw Myoo and Myow
roll into the space he had left and embrace each
other without wakening. He softly tapped a
message regretting his poor response to their
welcome and asking if one of their children
would return his pony to Dryhope common.
Then he dressed and left by a door onto the
veranda.

After a few steps on the shore path under
the trees his foot struck something soft. He
stopped and peered. There was not much light
in the sky but the path was pale enough to
show a small black body near the toe of his
right sandal and two or three others irregularly
placed on the path ahead: booby traps?
Stooping down he saw the nearest body
thrust a limb backward and lurch an inch
forward.
"Have more fun than I did," he told it and
walked on taking care where he placed his feet.
A minute later he said, "Whoever hears me may
like to know that my last remark was addressed

to a puddock. This is the night of the year when puddocks trek to the nearest fresh water for their annual nooky fair; but I doubt if *natural* history interests you Ms. Bitch. Are you listening? No need to speak; a tiny tinkle will do for yes, silence for no."

He listened and heard only leaves and water stirred by the pre-dawn breeze. The anger which had come to him on that path four hours earlier returned. In a sing-song voice he said, "I think I'll tell my friend Archie that someone's using a vast amount of public energy for a private seduction."

His wristcom worked as usual while he dialled the first Crook Cot digits, then it buzzed briefly like an angry wasp and the soft English voice said quickly, "What's a puddock?"

"I've forgotten the English word but the French is *crapaud*," said Wat, looking at a row of zeroes on the dial where the source of a message was usually indicated, "You sound like a woman who's just been wakened. There must be at least two of you listening."

"You are being tracked," said the voice, yawning slightly, "By a sensor beam linked to my wristcom. It shocked me awake with the first word you spoke."

"When will we meet?"

"Before you leave the path. Meanwhile I'll

amuse you with a suggestive poem.
The times are racked with birth pangs. Every hour
Brings forth some gasping Truth,
But Truth new born oft looks misshapen,
The terror of the household and its shame —
A Monster coiling in the mother's lap
That she would starve or strangle,

yet it breathes,
And suckled at a hundred half-clad breasts
Comes slowly to its form, staggers erect,
Smooths the rough ridges of its Dragon scales,
Changes to shining locks its snaky hair,
And moves transfigured into angel guise,
Welcomed by all who cursed its hour of birth.
— What do you think of that?"

"Not much. The stale imagery suggests the nineteenth century. Was it written by someone heralding socialism?"

"It was written by an American judge heralding fascism."

"Isms are the dullest bits of the historical midden. Why resurrect them?"

"Because we are about to give birth to the future and I am an agent of Shigalyovism which is organizing a political renaissance. But since sex comes before politics here is a wee song to cheer ye on your way, dearie."

He heard a burst of orchestral music and a Scottish male voice from the start of the

twentieth century sang —
"Keep right on to the end of the road,
Keep right on to the end!
Though the way be long
Let your heart be strong,
Keep right on round the bend!
Though you're tired, and weary,
Still journey on
Till you come to your happy abode,
Where all you love, you've been dreaming of,
Will be there — at the end — of the . . ."
"You're scaring the puddocks!" yelled Wat,
vainly trying to switch off his wristcom and
walk faster at the same time. He could see an
orange brightness low down among the trees
ahead. The voice went huskily seductive:
"You're a mean old daddy but you're out of
sight Wat honeyprick, come to momma you
sweetcocking motherfucker, come into me you
big bad world beater, I am the shining cunt at
the end of your personal tunnel."

The orange light came from the glowing
dome of a small tent with the shadow of a
reclining, beckoning figure inside. He stooped
and crawled in through an opening at the edge
of the path. She lay on a bank of pillows in the
rape-inviting position imposed on Jane Russell
by a millionaire who had owned some of

1944 Hollywood. She moaned, "Don't look at me like that you piece-a-shit!"
Two minutes later he lay gasping beside her after the fastest fuck of his life.

She said, "Do you know me now?"
He stared. Under the cosmetics (smudged now) of her archaic sexual mask he saw a young, very boyish face regard him alertly. He shook his head. She sighed and said, "I thought I was famous but of course you don't use public eyes."
He was too near to see her long body, slender waist, big breasts, but he felt them and was so disconcerted by her intense gaze (one blue eye, one brown) that he tried to lose it by again kissing and embracing but, "That's all for now," she said sitting upright, "Short brutish sex is the only sort revolutionaries have time for. When the present state withers away nobody will have time for the other sort either. A drink." Sitting cross-legged on the pillows she lifted a box from under one and took out a bottle of champagne and a glass. She said, "You still prohibit yourself alcohol?"

"Aye."

"Drink this."

She handed him a thermos flask which proved to contain scalding black coffee. He poured a cupful into the cap and let it cool, watching her closely and puzzling over what she had said about sex. Was she mad? She astonished him by how easily and quickly she fired the champagne cork out through the low doorway, and caught a fuming jet of liquor in the glass, and sipped it while putting the bottle back in the box and taking out a cigarette case. Nan's domestic actions had the same deft composure but not this alarming speed. He felt a thrumming in his blood, an expansion of breathing which were his usual reactions to danger. With relief he decided that his bodily chemistry was making him as alert as she. He was careful not to change his expression. He decided to say little and listen hard, yet she sat watching him and smiling at him and sipping champagne in such perfect silence that he was the first to speak.

"What's your name?"

"Puddock if you like me, Delilah if I'm a ball-breaker. Smoke one of these Hawaii Gold. It will clear your head and ease you into the plot." She spoke with the left side of her mouth while putting a lighter to a couple of slim brown tubes in the right. When he refused she unhesitatingly chucked one out through the entrance while inhaling the other, then sipped from the glass and in a voice that slid through several accents said, "Achtung Liebling! This is the situation. Many in the public eye are bored frantic by broadcasting the same old war games. The viewing public are also bored — that is why chieftains like your father have been bidding for attention by squandering more and more lives. The warriors too are bored. I won't remind you how, in a young girl's arms, you prayed for homes to be bombed and women to be mutilated. I'll repeat something said by a general of the old school six days ago."

She touched her wristcom and a moment later Wat heard Shafto say, "People are tired of the old strategies. In a month or three you and me should put our heads together and see if we can work out other new strategies — within the Geneva Conventions of course."

"Fuck the Global and Interplanetary Council for War Regulation Sitting in Geneva!" said the woman with startling violence, "For ten thousand years of civilization mankind put its most creative energies into warfare, breaking old rules and inventing new ones every century, killing greater and greater multitudes in a crescendo of holocausts which kept pace with the enormous expansion of humanity. The world leaders called it *progress* of course, though they usually found it wiser to pretend that warfare was a temporary part of it. The wisest knew it was an essential part. Why purse your lips? Do you think me a monster?"

"I think you're a clown," said Wat, shrugging, "That civilized way of living and fighting nearly wrecked the planet."

"I agree," she said, refilling her glass, "That the twentieth and twenty-first centuries played games that nearly destroyed everything animal but the cockroaches. Yes, a peaceful century of fighting-by-rule was needed to restore human resources. The eighteenth century was a bit like ours. European rulers feared the chaotic wars of an earlier age so their armies only fought at frontiers. Polite people toured each other's nations, visited each other's homes whether their governments were warring or not. Those Europeans thought they were safer than the Imperial Romans, but boom! 1789! The French Revolution! A new age of warfare started which spread competing nations to every part of the globe. The biggest nation of all, the Chinese, tried to keep out of that rat race so the cocky wee Europeans and Yanks pulled it apart. *Our* rational Utopia is about to go boom and fall apart too and you, Wat Dryhope, are the virus of the plague which is going to destabilize it. Prost, skol and slainte you world-fucker. I'll soon want more of you."

"You foul-mouthed big blethering nonsense!" said Wat, amused. She smiled unpleasantly and said, "If you used the public eye you would know that what happened in Ettrick yesterday is happening now on the sunny side of the globe. In the Americas and Asias scholars, gurus, gardeners and artists are crowding to their Warrior houses. Armies are doubling and trebling. The world's great new war hero, Wat Dryhope, came to soldiering late in life, why should every man not do it? Your coffee's getting cold."

Wat, thinking hard, sipped it then said, "That's no sign of instability! It just shows how widespread male boredom is. The commanders will cope by conferring with Geneva and devising new rules for bigger war games. A lot more men will die, of course, but even if three quarters of male humanity slaughter each other it won't destroy the modern state. The modern state depends on women minding their houses."

"Have you forgotten that I am a woman? I am also an agent of the Shigalyovite Revolution."

"You are an eloquent, erudite liar, Delilah

Puddock," said Wat, chuckling, "Tell me about Shigalyovism."

"You are a man I will enjoy humiliating, Wat Dryhope," said the woman dreamily inhaling her cigarette yet still watching him closely, "Shigalyov was a Russian who loved freedom and plotted against the Czar. He proved by algebra that freedom can only be fully enjoyed in a world where one tenth of the people are given unrestricted powers over the remaining nine tenths."

"The poor man must have been so obsessed with Czardom that Russian Communism was the only alternative he could imagine," said Wat, screwing the empty cap back on the flask, "Will your conspiracy bring back that?"

"O no, Russian Communism was dull and inefficient. We will recreate the system which overpowered it, *the competitive exploitation of human resources*."

"Are human resources people?"

"Of course, but when exploiting people it is best to think them a passive substance like oil or earth."

"You havenae said a word of practical sense," said Wat, suddenly noticing he was no longer alert. His thoughts, his words also were coming ponderously: "You can only exploit folk . . . who depend on you for essential things like

. . . food or ways of getting it . . . Landlords
and merchants used to do that by removing
food from folk who produced it . . . You could
then deal it out to them in such wee amounts
that . . . that poor folk grew too weak to grab
it for themselves, especially when you employed
a well-paid police force . . . Then . . . then
the producers would lick your boots and c
. . . cut each other's throats hoping you'll
give them enough to let their w . . . wea . . .
WEANS STAY ALIVE WHY'RE YE NODN
AN GIGGLIN?"
Sweating and trembling he fell back on the
pillows. She flung cigarette and glass out onto
the path (he heard it smash) and knelt upright
across his thighs.
"You really do understand political economy,"
she said, putting her hands beneath her breasts,
lifting them and smiling down on him between.
"That's all past," he whispered, appalled to feel
his penis swell, erect, yearn up to her while the
rest of him helplessly shivered. She said, "Time
for more, my wee Sssscottish Ressssource."
Caressing her nipples slowly with her thumbs
she crooned, *"The bright old day now dawns
again, the cry goes through the land, in
England there shall be dear bread — in
Ireland, sword and brand; and poverty, and
ignorance, shall swell the rich and grand,*

so rally round the rulers with the gentle iron hand, of the fine old English Tory days; hail to the coming time! Spurs on the dinnerplates! Guns before butter! If you had shared my champers and pot you would be enjoying this but the doctored coffee won't sssspoil *my* pleasure Ssssamson."

Grabbing his hair with both hands she eased herself down on him whispering, "*George Orwell said the future of humanity would be a jackboot continually stamping on a face. He was wrong. It's gonna be me continually fucking your brains out.*"

Wat obstinately closed his eyes. She opened them with her thumbs. He deliberately emptied his mind of thoughts and lost consciousness after some helpless, shameful intervals of pain and pleasure

and wakened still helpless and shivering but on his feet. He was upright because his arm was over the shoulder of a robust presence who also grasped him round the waist. There was a big brown animal nearby. Some pale blobs before him were probably faces.

"Careful, Colonel Dryhope! Take it easy sir!"
said Jenny's voice.

He was on the shore of Saint Mary's Loch
on a cold grey morning with sharp aches in his
head and testicles and muscles. Jenny was
supporting him. Nearby his father's horse,
Bucephalus, stood on the path under the trees,
sniffing among pebbles at broken glass and a
crushed cigarette. Women from Bowerhope
were in front of him. Myoo laid her hand
tenderly on his shoulder and said sadly, "Oh
Wattie lad, you look awfy sick."
"How came your clothes in that fankle?" asked
Myow beside her and Wat noticed his clothes
felt dirty and ill-fitting. He realized Delilah
Puddock must have put them on him while he
lay unconscious and before she removed the
tent. This provoked two feelings he knew to
be insane: gratitude so maudlin that it brought
tears to his eyes; a sadistic lust to punish her
so urgent that it made his testicles ache worse
than ever. He groaned and said, "I'm sick, aye,
but don't ask what happened. I need Kittock."
"There are many messages for you at the
Warrior house Colonel."
"Send them to Dryhope but first help me onto
this bloody big horse."

FIVE

THE HENWIFE

HE DISMOUNTED on Dryhope
common, stabled Bucephalus and went
through the garden without seeing a soul. He
was thankful but puzzled, then realized that if
Bowerhope had warned the Dryhope mother
of his filthy and disordered appearance she
would certainly have organized a party or
expedition to move the children where they
would not see him. She had also made the walls
of the house opaque except for a line of clear
portholes under the eaves. As he approached
the veranda she was waiting for him there and
said sternly, "What hit ye? Have ye been
pioneering in the woods? Is this the result of
alfresco fucking?"

"Aye, but not how ye think. Where are the
bairns?"

"Off to watch the circus being pitched on the hills round Selkirk. The aunts and a few grannies have gone with them."

Standing on the path beneath her he said, "I'm coming no nearer till nurses have seen me. Mibby I'm infected with something."

"Aye? Well, they're waiting for you."

He walked round the path to the infirmary door. It was ajar. He mounted the veranda and entered.

Two nieces, a sister and a cousin swiftly undressed him and were shocked by the sight of his body. They said, "Naebody in Ettrick makes love like that!" and, "Were you playing soldiers with a queer man, Wat?"

"No."

"Was it a gangrel lass?"

"No."

"Was it a circus woman?"

"Mibby. She said she was famous but I didnae ken her. Be quick with this."

One cleaned his body and put lotions on the wounds. The others took samples of his breath, blood, lymph, urine and (by an exertion which almost had him screaming) semen. They analyzed the samples and keyed the results into the network while he was shaved and massaged by hands which expertly avoided the bites and bruises. One told him, "Your brother Joe is a lot cheerier. Annie Craig Douglas visited him last night. She's still with him."

"Good."

"She says her mother sent her — Nan, ye ken? — but I think Annie would like to see you."

"I'll see naebody till I've seen Kittock."

"You can see her as soon as you've dressed and had your medicine," said another handing him a diagnostic printout.

It said Wat Dryhope's excellent constitution had been exhausted by at least nine days of intense muscular and nervous exertion, by opiate overdose from a cocktail of caffeine-flavoured chloroform water plus heroin plus alcohol plus cocaine plus L-dopa aphrodisiac, also by a common and harmless throat infection which only afflicted the exhausted. For the exhaustion it prescribed a fortnight of mild activity, sauna baths and massage; for the narcotic poisoning, detoxification with naloxone and total avoidance of all stimulants including caffeine; for the throat infection, a syrup of squill liquid extract and capsicum tincture, one spoonful after meals. A nurse went to order these medicines from the powerplant. In a puzzled way Wat re-read the diagnosis.

"A few hours ago I was in the worst fever of
my life," he said, frowning, "My heart was
hammering and the sweat lashing off me, but I
don't remember coughing. Are ye *sure* I've
just a throat infection?"

"No, Wat, we're too ignorant, but the network
is sure. The network has records of every virus
that ever mutated naturally, along with those
invented by murderous governments and
business corporations in the bad old days. It
knows all viruses that have evolved on the
satellites and the planets, all viral mutations
which could possibly happen in the last three
weeks and next ten days. You're *safe*, Wattie.
Your fever was a sober body's healthy reaction
to bad drugs in your coffee. I hope you gave
the bitch as good as you got."

"Here's a *billet doux* from her!" cried one of
his nieces triumphantly, returning from Wat's
room with clean clothing and a rainbow-
coloured ticket which she waved above her
head, "I found this and a book about shaking
the world while emptying his dirty pockets. It's
for tonight's circus and on the back it says —"

"Gie's it!" yelled Wat so fiercely that she stuck
out her tongue at him, threw the clothes into
his lap, dropped the ticket on top. He lifted it
and read with the other nurses peering over
and round his shoulders.

Cher Liebling!
I will never forget the maddening
sweetness of your caresses. Dressed in flame
tonight I will again be yr
slave after the
big show.
D.P.

Someone asked him what the initials meant and
he said they wouldnae believe him if he told.
He spoke absent-mindedly because the words
on the card filled him with a murderous desire
for Delilah Puddock. Someone asked if she was
a circus artist, a gopher or a camp follower.
He cried, "I've telt ye I don't ken a thing about
her! I just ken that I'm going to —"
Their startled faces silenced him. He saw his
hands clutching the air before him as though
throttling a neck.
"Lassies," he said plaintively, "I'm hungry. My
wame thinks my throat's cut."
They brought him powsoudie, drummock,
kebbuck and farle. He ate it and dressed.

Kittock had no modern intelligence
communicators so he went through the garden
to the old tower near the duck pond. The smoke
of her oven trickled up through bushes on the
ruined top. She was not in the goose field or
poultry runs and as usual (he thought with a

smile) the tower door was locked against him. She might be entertaining a gangrel. On a scrap of paper he wrote, "Wat is home, mother, and badly needs you," slipped it under the door, returned to the house,

and entering his room suddenly saw it was too small for a grown man. When he had returned from the stars, and found it kept for him, and realized the women had foreseen he would return, he had been so grateful that he had refused offers of a bigger room. The only change since infancy was a bed which now covered half the floor, also a new telecom with commander facilities — the mother must have ordered and installed it as soon as she heard of his colonelization. The screen showed names of many who wished to speak with him but none was Delilah Puddock. A thick sheaf of pink, blue and violet printed sheets had issued from it. He could not face them so made the outer wall transparent and was soothed a little by the familiar view: a garden with a tower holding the wisest person he knew, the loch and hills beyond the tower

under a cloudy April sky which was brightening
to a fine afternoon. With a faint cough the
telecom spat a rainbow-coloured message onto
the sheaf. Its print was too eye-catching to be
ignored.

PROFESSOR DOGBITCH Z. CELLINI
Virtuoso Assoluto of the
COSMOPOLITAN CLOUD CIRCUS
invites
COLONEL WAT DRYHOPE
*Commander of the Ettrick Warriors
and Prime Instigator of the New Era of
Military Power and Poetry*
to be
GUEST OF HONOUR
At a Grand Banquet Breakfast for
ARTISTS, HEROES, COMMANDERS
*Attending the Dusk-to-Dawn
Never-to-be-Repeated Cloud Circus
Production of*
HOMAGE TO ETTRICK

*A Four Act Evolutionary Opera
Hymning Creative Strife From The
Big Bang to The Battle of
The Ettrick Standard!*
ORIGINAL TEXTS BY
*Homer, Virgil, Ovid, Dante, Milton,
Goethe, Tolstoy, T. S. Eliot,
MacDiarmid, Hamish Henderson*
et cetera;
ORIGINAL MUSIC BY
*Carver, Haydn, Beethoven, Berlioz,
Wagner, Verdi, Stravinsky,
Hamish MacCunn*
et cetera;
ORIGINAL CLOUD EFFECTS BY
*Rubens, Tiepolo, Delacroix, Turner,
Shanks . . .*

Impatiently Wat scanned the print for the name
of a living woman and saw Alauda Magna was
Choral Synthesizer, Cathleen na Houlihaun was

Cloud Choreographer and the mirages had been
designed by Lulu Dancy. Under these was a
guest list of over three hundred commanders
and famous fighters from all round the globe.
Lust for Delilah Puddock, the honour of his
clan, personal vanity now pulled him so
strongly toward the circus that he instinctively
knew it would be wrong to go. Welcoming
escorts, loud cheering, handshakes with other
celebrities would inevitably turn him into a
posturing, smirking ornament — into a something used for other people's benefit. To find
why he had been called *Instigator of the New
Era* he switched his telecom to the public
eye.

Several housewives, one weeping, said the
mobilization epidemic infecting most of the
world's males was a crazy and dangerous fad.
An equal number of young women were shown
who expressed pride that their brothers or
lovers would face death for the glory of their
clan.
"Like the crowds of men swarming to their local
Warrior houses, most people in the public eye
are responding euphorically," said a public eye
announcer euphorically, "Commanders everywhere predict a new age of more challenging
war games played on a scale of almost historical

proportions. They also insist that this is no cause for alarm. The Geneva Conventions will not be contravened though war game rules may have to be redrawn."

Wat was alarmed by how many people said there was no cause for alarm. He watched Wolfgang Hochgeist with a globe of the world showing the spread of the epidemic from its origin in Ettrick. The least infected areas were Tibet, Ireland, Switzerland, Scandinavia and Italy. Most of the worst infected had military histories. In Japanese, German and French speaking lands the armies trebled, in the British Isles and North America they more than quadrupled. The big surprise was Canada, where fighting men had multiplied by six. Hochgeist daringly suggested that the Japanese, German and French had been slightly inoculated against militarism by historical recollections of disaster; Britain and the former U.S.A. were more prone to it because of former victories; Canada was worst infected because as a historical nation it had a less secure identity for which it was now compensating.

"The persistence and evolution of national military attitudes through generations for whom nationality has not been operational is interesting but not alarming," said Hochgeist, "Since soldiers will not be fighting to enrich their homes future warfare will remain unpolitical."

Wat switched to another channel and found an amicable discussion between Hinchinbrook, commander of the East Anglian Alliance, and Winesburg, North America's most popular fighter since Stormin' Norman. The alert and boyish Englishman was obviously talking hard to impress the famous veteran.

"The primitive armies of yesterday — and I mean *precisely* the yesterday of twenty-four hours ago — were single regiments. This wonderful new influx means every general must divide his force into three, four, five new regiments, so we will require a whole new hierarchy of command."

"Or an *old* hierarchy of command?" said Winesburg, smiling.

"Of course! How clever of you to notice. Yes, we will have to bring back the highly unpopular sergeant major."

"And commanding officers will lead less risky lives, if you don't mind a battle-scarred old veteran saying so."

"Quite right! More brain work, less cut and thrust."

"What do you think now of the global and interplanetary referendum called by Geneva,

General Hinchinbrook?"

"What do *you* think of it General Winesburg?"

"Out of date?"

"Utterly out of date. I don't mind keeping the Boys' Brigades in reserve because with these thousands of other lives to play with we don't need them. But it's absurd to confine battles of the scale we now anticipate to two days! Why not a fortnight? Plenty of room to manoeuvre in that. And this fuss about *standards* also seems outmoded. What the world's armies now need — and what our families viewing us from home deserve — is a more inspiring object to struggle for. Last week a great Scottish soldier called his standard *a pole with a tin chicken on top*. I was shocked, I confess. I now see he had the right idea."

"Have you another object to fight for in mind?"

"None. Not the faintest. But in six months — not more than six months — we'll be commanding whole new companies of troops just raring to go. I dare say we'll have thought of something better by then."

"Would you mind saying a word about the manoeuvring of large new armies on common land for whole fortnights?" said a public eye chairman, "Won't that play havoc with the migration of gangrels? Not with all of them everywhere, of course, but many of them

sometimes?"
"Some havoc, no doubt," said Hinchinbrook
with a pleasant smile, "But we are many and
they are few. I'm sure they'll manage to adapt.
Besides, they stink. There is nothing to be
alarmed about as long as our houses are safe."

Wat blanked the screen and gloomily
pondered the fact that every general in the
world would soon command a new army of
beginners, most of them bigger than his
because they lived in more peopled places. He
had another fit of wanting Delilah Puddock.
He wanted to tie her up and torture her until
she told him exactly what she was trying to do;
he was also disgusted with himself because he
knew she must have foreseen that reaction. He
kicked his shoes off, lay on the bed and tried
not to want her by remembering other women
he had passionately wanted. Their only
similarity was that none had passionately
wanted him.

He had staggered after the henwife as soon as
he learned to walk because she was small, aloof,

and unlike the comforting big-bosomed grannies and thin energetic ones. She only visited the house for the morning service, always ordering two sacks of grain and a book. She had a pocket for the book but he insisted on carrying it, trotting beside her when she crossed the garden to the poultry yard with a sack under each arm. After feeding the geese, hens and chickens she firmly took the book back, entered the ancient tower and shut him out. No other granny had a door which could be locked from inside. It was the only wooden door in Dryhope and he hated it, kicked and screamed at it, pounded it with his fists, threw stones at it and occasionally butted it with his head until the Dryhope mother came and carried him home. After what seemed years but was maybe less than a month the upper half of the door opened inward. Kittock leaned her folded arms on top of the lower half, looked down on him with interest and said, "Will you keep doing that till I let ye in?"

"Aye."

"Even if I never let ye in?"

"Aye."

"If you hold on to me you'll have a lonely life, Wattie. I don't like weans."

"I don't care."

"O, if you understand that cheeriness is not

man's chief end, come in."

The tower wall was so thick that the doorway seemed a tunnel. It led to the living-room, a cavernous vault with a plank floor, a big flat-topped stove in the middle, several chairs and a table. The stove was called the Aga. Above it stood a giant bed whose leg-posts were seven feet high and nine inches square. It had a ladder to climb in by and a low plank wall to prevent rolling out. From floor to ceiling the walls were hidden by shelves packed with every size of book, some in good condition but most appearing to have been often read by people with dirty hands. She led him across this chamber and up a dank spiral stair. They reached to a vault shaped like the one below. It was loud with croodling pigeons and had a thick carpet of feathers and bird shit.

"The doocot," she said, leading him higher. They emerged between broken walls on an open space where brambles, birks and an osier bush sprouted. Wat, looking out across the sunlit loch, had never been so high. He felt as high as the hills. After a moment Kittock said, "I am the henwife because I'm too selfish to be a housewife, too feart to be a gangrel. We should all be gangrels. Will I make ye one Wattie? I know their ways."

"No."

"Their lives are short but never dreich because they see more than settled folk — they can only feed and keep warm by seeing more. They have added reading to their old skills of song and story-telling. Some are still Christians — it adds zest to their swearing. Most are fiercely monogamous and often unfaithful. They need no powerplants and telecoms because the world is their house. Would you not like the world for your house Wattie?"

"It's too big, Kittock."

"Gangrels don't think so. Do you promise never to try and stop me doing what I enjoy?"

"Aye."

"Do you promise not to ask more than two questions a day?"

"Aye."

"Do you promise to go on playing in the garden with your nephews and nieces?"

"Aye."

"Then stay for a while and I'll teach ye to read."

She had taught him to read very fast, he thought, remembering how shocked he had been when the lessons stopped. She had promised to cuddle him all night when he had read her a Rudyard Kipling story aloud from start to finish. In bed she always lay with her back to him; he hated that so worked hard and read the story aloud perfectly.

"Good," she said briskly, "My teaching days are over. Now you can teach yourself."

"But you'll cuddle me all night?"

"Aye, for the first and last time. You should cuddle lassies of your own age."

Because it was the first and last time he couldn't enjoy being cuddled by her that night. He told her so.

"Good!" she said pleasantly, "Neither of us is being used as a doll."

"Are you my mother, Kittock?"

"Mibby. I had a wheen of bairns before I tired of housework. I was good at childbirth but never nursed the gets for more than a week because I didnae like small thoughtless animals. Luckily there are a lot of women who do. Folk who cannae talk bore me. I went to the stars to hear a brainier class of talker."

"Why did ye come back?"

"The talkers up there are all specialists."

"I hope you're my mother, Kittock."

"It doesnae matter *who* is your mammy and daddy, you're the world's son, my man, born into the world's house, and if it's too big for you, leave it and crawl into a satellite or a crater with a roof over it on a dead world. Ask the grannies who your mammy is. They told you

about your daddy because boys are supposed
to feel safer with a manly pattern ahead of them,
just as girls are supposed to feel safer with a
mother. Mibby they do feel safer but it's idol-
worship or doll-cuddling just the same. The
only pattern we should learn to follow is the
one that grows inside us. You have to look in,
not out to find that."

"I don't know what ye mean Kittock."

"Then forget it."

He had never asked the grannies who his
mother was in case she was not Kittock at all.

There was every kind of book on Kittock's
shelves, many with pictures. He found one with
tiny engravings of many naked women and a
few men wearing curly wigs, knee breeches,
embroidered dressing-gowns and buckled
shoes. The men seemed to own a vast palace
where they used the women as furniture and
ornaments. The text was in words he could
not read.

"What does *play-sir dam-our* mean, Kittock?"

"Pleasure of love, in French."

"Will you teach me French?"

"No. Learn it through a telecom in the big
house. Contact a French boy who wants to learn
English. Show him that book and ask him to
explain."

"I wish you had a telecom."

"I don't want to learn another language."

"You could watch films."

"It would waste my mind."

He wanted to ask why, but it would have been his third question that day. He watched her hard and expectantly instead. She sighed and said, "When a lot of folk watch something on a screen they all see the same thing. What a damnable waste of mind! Readers bring books to life by filling the stories with voices, faces, scenery, ideas the author never dreamed of, things from their *own* minds. Every reader does it differently."

"So when you and me read *The Cat That Walked by Itself* we read a different story?" said Wat, disliking the idea.

"Exactly!" said Kittock with great satisfaction.

"Can a man say a sensible word?" said a fat, thickly bearded gangrel sitting in a chair near the Aga where he had been examining a book, "You undervalue intercourse between *people*, Kitty my love. Yes, in Hegelian terms every book is a thesis to which each and every reader's reaction — no matter how enthusiastic! — is antithesis and uniquely private. This would turn us into Babylonian chaos or a swarm of solipsistic monads if natural garrulity did not make us chorally symphonic. We mingle our private and divergent responses to what delights or exasperates us, thus instigating a plurality of new syntheses. Glory be to God, you're a lovely woman, Kitty. Let a man tip another drop of real stuff into your glass."

"Ignore him, Wat," said Kittock amiably, "None of his words are sensible except a few at the end."

Gangrels visited the tower to return and borrow books, usually bringing a hare or salmon for the larder, sometimes a load of peats or logs for the Aga. Wat hated them because he wanted Kittock to himself. He hated the fat man most because he had come early, seemed perfectly at home and showed no sign of going away. Kittock had produced two glasses which the fat man kept filling from a labelless bottle of clear liquid. At one point he asked Kittock, "Should a man offer a drop of real stuff to your solemn young husband here?"

"Aye, but he'll refuse. He hates you."

The man asked Wat politely, "Is she telling the truth?"

"Aye."

"Ah well, here's a health to you anyway."

Later they were joined by another gangrel just as bad: a small thin one with a deeply wrinkled brow, moustache so bushy that it hid his mouth, a sack from which he removed another bottle of real stuff, a copy of *Catch 22*, rabbits, birds, potatoes, onions and a turnip which he suggested would make a good game stew. Kittock started preparing it. The men exchanged tobacco pouches, filled their pipes, filled their glasses again and discussed whether ten thousand years of civilization should be called The Dark Ages because of their greed and cruelty, or The Middle Ages because they had achieved some splendid things. The discussion lasted throughout the afternoon, through a meal of game stew, through the evening until long after nightfall. During it Wat heard so many people confidently quoted that he thought the gangrels had recently met Socrates, Pericles, Voltaire, Frederick of Prussia, Pushkin, Czar Nicholas, James Kelman and Margaret Thatcher in remote cities. In Dryhope house he sometimes saw films of people living in cities, so did not know they had disappeared. And all the time Kittock listened closely to the men with quiet amusement which infuriated Wat because *he* could not amuse her that way. Without bidding anyone goodnight at last he climbed the ladder to bed and, despite the loud voices below, fell asleep without undressing.

And was shaken awake by Kittock saying,

"Home to your aunties, Wat! Home to your aunts!"

There was a smile on her face giving it a youthful beauty he had never seen before. When he understood what she meant he yelled, "No!" and clung to the side of the bed.

"Help me men!" she cried gaily, "Up here, Tiger Tim. Stay below and catch him, Desperate Dan."

She and the small man lifted him and dropped him screaming into the arms of the fat man who carried Wat to the door, pushed him out, slammed and locked and bolted it behind him. The night was warm, a full moon in the sky. He rushed at the door, banged it uselessly with his shoulder, kicked it, hammered with his fists and yelled furiously for minutes on end till he was suddenly drenched by a big cold lump of water. It had been tipped from a pail by the fat man who, looking down from the broken tower top, said, "Moderate your transports you misfortunate wee bastard! It's a big bed but there's only room for two men when Kitty goes wild."

Then he was being led back to his first home by a mother who said softly, "Poor Wat, poor Wat, why did ye attach yourself to *her?* Tonight you'll sleep with me."

"No!"

"Well I'll put you in with Joe — he likes you."

"No!"

"Then where can I put ye, Wattie? Who in this great big house do you want to sleep with? I can arrange it with anyone for tonight, maybe for longer. Peggy is loving. She's ten and plump and likes wee lads."

Snatching his hand from hers he hardened every muscle till his body vibrated with tension and roared, *"Can a man not have a bed of his own?"*

"O yes," she said, smiling sadly down on him, "A man can have a bed of his own."

A day later he saw Kittock at the morning service and glared at her. She smiled and shrugged back. His feelings then were exactly what he felt now for Delilah Puddock. Before returning from the stars he could not think of Kittock without pain; afterward he was as glad to see her as any of the rest.

Yes, he had come to this small room at the age of five. Most children were given a bigger room when they left their chosen granny at that age, sharing it with two or three others. They slept, played, squabbled together until puberty, when each wanted, and was given, a room of their own to entertain privately invited guests.

Wat had never wanted another room. He wanted attractive nieces and young aunts to stand outside his little room and say timidly, "Wat, O Wattie, please let me in."

He found cruel pleasure in imagining their sufferings when they heard him say very coldly and casually, "Leave me alone, I'm busy."

Unluckily the only girl who had begged to enter his room was a tall awkward eleven-year-old lassie from Mountbenger who visited him when he was nine. She had been so awkward and unattractive — so like himself — that there was no satisfaction in keeping her out. She had sat for hours on his floor but eventually stopped coming because he answered her questions with monosyllables, said nothing else to her, never looked at her and went on reading or playing with his screen as if alone. Later he heard she had grown into a uniquely intelligent and attractive woman, so her dull remarks to him had been caused by shyness. He still fantasized about excluding women who loved him. When twelve he had refused an offer of a bigger room, saying he would soon be leaving for the satellites as soon as possible so must get used to cramped spaces. He bitterly enjoyed the sorrowing wonder with which the mother heard this crisp, quiet statement. It had proved he was cared for. But those he most wanted

had never cared much for him. Kittock had not
wanted him near her. Nan was more of a mother
than an equal. Annie had talked to him as if
she was an older sister. He had certainly loved
them but none (except Kittock, perhaps) had
occupied his mind as wholly as the woman in
the tent who had treated him with absolute
contempt.

"Why am I a perverse bugger?" he whispered then
noticed someone on the veranda watching him.

It was Kittock. She nodded without smiling
and turned and walked back to the tower. He
put his shoes on and scribbled a note: *A political
matter — someone you do not know is listening
to us*.

His room lacked a door onto the veranda.
He caught up with her in the living-room
library he had not visited for over twenty years.
She stood facing him, hands clasped before her
in perfect silence. He said, "You're angry?"
She nodded.
"Why?"
She took his first note from her pocket, showed

it to him, lifted a plate from the Aga and dropped it inside saying, "I never mothered you."

He humbly shrugged his shoulders and handed her the second note. She read it, looked at him, smiled and burned that too. She said kindly, "Sit down Wattie. If false folk are listening the truth cannae hurt you. You arenae false."

It was what he wanted to hear.

"Are ye sure?" he said, thankfully sitting, "I met a very bad woman last night, Kittock."

"I think ye met a woman who was bad to you, Wattie."

"If what she said is right she wants to be bad to everyone and I love her, Kittock!" said Wat with a wild chuckle, "There's been naething like me since José fell for Carmen. I'm corrupted!"

She brewed and served camomile tea while he talked, then she sat opposite and gave him such full attention that he felt as safe at home with her as when he was three. She asked questions which helped him recall details, like the colour of Delilah's eyes. He also told her the news he had gathered through the telecom, growing excited about it.

"Surely there's more than one of her, Kittock? The public eye presenters and telecom gurus and commanders broadcasting just now all seem part of her conspiracy, but so do I — the worst part. An hour ago a veteran strategist called me *the spearhead of a great new movement restoring manly courage to its ancient prestige* — he predicted that in a year we'll be battling in leagued armies as big as those of the defunct nations and based on the same territories. *Weapons and war rules must be modified for larger areas of manoeuvre,* he said, *but only the commons will be seriously encroached upon.* A woman asked if this meant future battles would not only be fought on the commons, but also for them. He said *Why not? Territorial instincts will add zest to manly contests and in no way endanger our houses.* Why are so many so sure of this? Why are only a few women worried about it? I must fight this daftness —"

"Fight it?"

"Speak against it. Every commander in Scotland will be at a banquet after the circus tonight with nearly a hundred foreign champions. As guest of honour I'll be expected to make a speech. What if I tell the world that there is a conspiracy against the safety of our homes?"

"You will sound like a quotation from a history book," mused Kittock, "At first the whole audience will think you a fearmongering maniac from the worst period of human history. Then your sincerity will move folk who like you, and others who also fear the effect of the bigger armies, to start a crusade, a witch hunt, a police force to denounce or arrest plotters. The folk any such force arrested or threatened to arrest would mostly be innocent, of course. The new police force, like previous ones, would become the evil it was created to prevent and would provoke a resistance exactly like it. That would delight the puddock you met in the wood."

"Shall I kill her and then myself, Kittock?"

"I believe she would like that too, Wattie. Finish your tea while I think."

He sipped lukewarm tea, watched her ponder and relaxed into the comfort of the high-backed armchair. Since explaining his problem to her he was enjoying a pleasant drowsiness. The colour of a winking light on his wristcom showed three people had left urgent messages and a fourth wanted to talk to him at once. He let the winking light hypnotize him into shallow sleep which suddenly deepened

and banquet, Wat," said Kittock loudly. He yawned and muttered, "I didnae catch that."

"Don't go to that circus and banquet. Don't even speak to these people, let Jenny do it for you. Tell him you've a viral infection, but don't say you cannae go. Say you won't go, and mean it."

He took the ticket from his pocket, re-read the message, sighed and said, "All right mother, though it will be hard. Every bit of me but my common sense hungers for that woman."

"Stand firm. Hold on to your common sense and she'll come to you," said Kittock grimly, "I won't let you out of my sight today, tonight or tomorrow, Wat. Stop looking excited! She can only harm ye."

"I told you I'm corrupted, mother," said Wat with a despairing smile, "I know she can only harm me so my only hope is she needs me to do it to. Why are ye sure she'll come?"

"I'll tell you when we've seen the great-grannies of Dryhope," said Kittock, standing, "Come! We must tell them everything."

"Why?" asked Wat, perplexed, "What use are a wheen of old housewives to anybody but the bairns they care for? I ken they like knowing all about everything but gossip won't save the world — or save me either."

"Sometimes you have fewer brains than a headless hen Wat Dryhope! You always thought too little of the women who bred and nursed you because you wanted danger, not safety — that's why you fell in love with me, and history books, and going to the stars, and warfare, and with Delilah Puddock. I wish I could have made you a gangrel, Wat. That life has all the healthy danger a sane man needs and no time for communal crazes and elite conspiracies. Among settled people it's the great-grannies who stop these things becoming dangerous. Their gossip has been the only government and police the world has needed for more than a century — if you're ignorant of that then you don't know what keeps modern society stable. If *she* is as ignorant as you in that respect (and she may be, you and she were very alike) we can stop her doing much damage."

"Who are you talking about?"

"The bonny, merciless puddock you met in the woods, Lulu Dancy, who was sweet on you when you were wee."

Wat jumped up and walked to and fro saying, "That scrawny, lanky thing? She wasnae a Lulu — they cried her . . . What was it . . ?"

"Meg Mountbenger. You paid her no attention so she came to me, asked all about you and read the books you read. I got her hooked on books. She borrowed more than anyone I ever knew, history, art, poetry and novels. A very clever lass she became and a good looker with it, but she was scunnered by the Ettrick lads after you and didnae care much for her aunts and grannies either. She became an artist and went to the stars. She was one of the team designing the hollow world, K20, but she loved sounds and appearances more than solid forms so changed her name to what it is now, returned to earth and joined Cellini's Cloud Circus last year — what's suddenly right with ye, Wattie?" With tears on his cheeks he said hoarsely, "I've never been happier. She needs me like I need her! There was hatred in what she did with me last night but nothing calculating, nothing political! It's a miracle that she's needed me all these years. I'll go to her."

Kittock grasped his hands and tried to keep him seated saying, "And she wasnae false when she said she wanted to restore poverty and greedy governments! Does her brand of nooky mean more to ye than the proper feeding of the world's bairns? The safety of our sisters, aunts and grannies? The happiness of Annie, Nan and your other kind sweethearts?"

"She cannae hurt them," said Wat impatiently pulling his hands free, getting up and going toward the door, "And I'll stop her if she tries

to, that's a promise Kittock."
On an agonized note Kittock cried, "*She's a
neo-sapience Wat!*"
He stared then asked how she knew.
"Guess," she said, smiling mournfully.
"You're one too?"
She nodded.

After a moment he spoke casually, like a man
prepared to spend a few more minutes with a
stranger. He was pleased to see this hurt her.
"When I was wee you told me the earth is the
seed bed of the universe — that folk who choose
immortality must leave the earth to prevent
overcrowding. Immortals break that rule?"
"I'm no immortal now," said Kittock humbly,
"I shogged off the insanity of rejuvenation
when I returned to earth. I was sixty years
abroad in the universe before admitting how
much I hated eternity and infinity, how much I
needed the world's wonderful big smallness.
The Dryhope grannies (some of them my
daughters) let me sneak back to this outhouse
where I crowd nobody and take nothing from
the powerplant but poultry food and books for
the gangrels. But Meg Mountbenger is another
kind of woman altogether. She's also your . . ."

A rushing noise like distant wind had been

coming nearer and suddenly surrounded the
tower with a deafening, steady roar. The door
at the foot of the spiral stairs burst open, a
blast of warm air came out carrying a cloud of
dust, feathers and four pigeons who tumbled
and fluttered overhead before settling in
window slits and book shelves. Wat and
Kittock, partly blinded by dust, rushed to push
the door shut but before they reached it the
pressure of the blast eased and the roaring,
though still continuous, lessened enough for
the noise of hearty male voices and descending
footsteps to be heard from above.

The first to enter was a young lad in Boys'
Brigade uniform who cried, "Wattie, Wattie,
we got the standard, we got the standard!"
It was Sandy, Wat's brother. Behind him a bulky,
magnificent figure in the full dress uniform of
a Northumbrian commander stooped to get his
plumed helmet under the lintel. It was General
Shafto looking so robustly, serenely cheerful
that Wat felt happier at the mere sight of him.
Shafto turned his grin from Wat onto Kittock,
saluted her and said, "Forgive the rude

intrusion, madam, but we have come here on urgent warrior business, having failed to contact the Ettrick commander by any other method. Colonel Dryhope! My good friend and best enemy! Your carriage awaits upstairs with Archie Crook Cot in full control. Since the entire Northumbrian command were coming north for the shindig at Selkirk tonight (yes, even old Dodds — he's quite got over his huffs with you) I decided to return with your standard bearers, so here we are to collect the guest of honour and man of the moment."

"He's not going to the circus," said Kittock and Wat was puzzled by her appearance. She no longer looked calm and wise but small and frantic like a frightened child.

"Forgive me for disagreeing madam, but he must! The circus cannot start without him! World champions are waiting to shake your hand, Wat Dryhope — Inongo, Winesburg and Pingwu, to name but a few. Commanders of great new recently created military leagues are here to shake your hand — Sheer Khan of Mongolia, Jack Ripper of Texas, Siegfried Krawinkel of the Fifth Reich. Every commander in Scotland is waiting to shake your hand — yes, Scotland will be a nation again and who but Wat Dryhope is fit to lead it? By gum, the Scots and Sassenachs can look forward to some

grand scrimmages again! A whole galaxy of
public eyeballs is also waiting outside but we
won't pay any attention to *them*. Come
upstairs Wattie!"

With pursed lips Wat had been smiling,
nodding, almost laughing at what Shafto said
yet he did not go at once. Part of him knew he
was being swept away by other people's wills
and that nobody should let themselves be swept
away. He looked at Kittock. She stared back
and shook her head in a slight, definite
negation. He suddenly knew that *not* going
would be the greatest and truest act of his life
but Shafto, chuckling, put a warm friendly hand
on his shoulder and said, "Why should a hero
like you skulk away from his comrades like
Achilles did? Achilles' lovely bedmate had been
snapped from him by the commanding officer
but YOU are the supreme commander here and
the lovely and famous Lulu Dancy awaits your
command in the flying bedstead upstairs. Go
to her! Besides, Colonel Dryhope, your life is
partly mine! I saved it a week ago! Tonight I
insist that you do as *I* want. I order you to stop
being a damned dour reticent Scot and for once
enjoy yourself!"

So Wat went to the circus after all.

NOTES
& GLOSSARY
EXPLAINING
OBSCURITIES

PROLOGUE BY A HERO'S MOTHER

Page IX

scunnered = a shrinking recoil more intense than *disgusted*. It derives from the noun *sickener* or *scunner*.

dreich = grey and dull; cold and dismal.

Page X

snibbing = latching; bolting; locking.

uisge beatha = Gaelic for aqua vitae or water of life; a spirit obtained by distillation from a mash of cereal grains saccharified by the diastase of malt; otherwise known as whisky or Scotch.

Page XI

ramfeezle = muddle; confuse; exhaust.

Page XIII

tholed = suffered, endured or been afflicted with pain, grief et cetera.

bumbazing = perplexing; stupifying.

Page XIV

malagroozed = injured; hurt.

clanjamfries = miscellaneous assemblies.

Page XV

lang-nebbed = long-nosed; over-intellectual; seeming wiser than is the case.

Page 3.
Five commanders ... with ... deeply scarred faces.
Since medals were as obsolete as monarchs and presidents who had awarded them scars were now the only outward sign of a soldier's experience. Many senior officers rejected medical treatment which would heal their faces completely, but unlike German student duellists of the late nineteenth century did not invite medical treatment which would make the scars more conspicuous.

Page 7.
An epoch when most men are over six feet tall.
In the historical era good feeding and healthy exercise were often a perquisite of the officer class, whose average height, health and lifespan was usually greater than those who did not inherit wealth. In the nineteenth and twentieth centuries some scientists attributed such class differences to heredity: if the difference was genetic no political movement to better the lives of the badly fed could succeed. Yet in less than a century the average height of white Australians came to equal the average height of the British officer class, though at that time most white Australians were descended from poor people the British officer class had evicted.

Page 10.
bairns = infants, young folk, children or

offspring. Of Teutonic and Scandinavian origin, this word was widespread in England as well as Scotland before the 18th century. Shakespeare and Swift used it.

loons = young people, usually male, of a mischievous, rascally, sexually over-active or violent character; also used as an affectionate disparagement of someone the speaker likes or of the speaker himself. Natives of Forfar liked being called Forfar loons; it was the preferred nickname of that town's football team.

Page 11.

When your wounds heal join the veterans and Boys' Brigade in the Warrior house where you will be the only officers . . . Teach the Ettrick youngsters how to avoid them.

There were no private soldiers in modern armies. The lowest ranks were the Boys' Brigades which were seldom allowed to fight before the age of sixteen. Those who survived their first war and remained in the army at once became officers with full voting rights.

Page 13.

The Ettricks pull on their helmets and form a circle.

The helmets contained the only electronic equipment modern armies allowed themselves: earphones through which soldiers could hear their commander's voice on a wavelength

inaudible to anyone else.
Page 20.
whins = gorse or furze, a prickly flowering evergreen shrub that thrives throughout Europe and Africa in thin or stony soils.
Page 21.
The only signs of battle on the moorland slopes were some gangrels collecting scattered swords, helmets, shields.
gangrels = tinkers, tramps, vagabonds, vagrants, gipsies, nomads of no fixed abode. The earliest kind of humanity were of this sort and wandered around the land for millennia in small family groups, improvising tools and shelter, gathering and consuming their food as they went. In some countries they acquired sheep and goats which they drove before them. The early Jews and Arabs were this sort of folk. When some early gangrels settled and started farming, weaving and making clay pots those who still moved between them became the first traders. Increasing settlement produced city states, empires and vast civilizations so gangrels inside their boundaries lived by migrant labour such as fruit picking, horse trading, scavenging, mending kettles, conjuring and making music. On the vast grasslands of northern Eurasia travelling nations of horse-riding herdsmen grew strong enough to counter-attack the

settled lands of China pressing from the east
and Rome from the west. Their attacks broke
the Roman empire into the Christian nations
of a new Europe, for the invading horsemen
could not have gainfully managed the towns
and territories they conquered without help
from a priesthood who read and wrote. Their
attacks gave China also a new ruling dynasty.
When such gangrels became landlords their
travelling days ended, except when they raided
their neighbours.

Governments of the historical era who
wanted to distract public attention from their
greed or uselessness usually went to war, but
when war with outsiders seemed too dangerous
or expensive they declared war on a part of
those they ruled, and for at least two thousand
years Jews and gangrels were the traditional
victims. Between 1942 and 44 the German
government tried to kill all the gipsies and Jews
in Europe and killed about six million of each.
In 1990 the British Home Secretary (a
politician employed to protect British
households) accompanied a police attack on a
camp of gangrels on the ancient common of
Glastonbury. Men and women were clubbed,
their mobile homes smashed with truncheons,
and next day the British Prime Minister

announced in Parliament, "I see it as my duty to make life hard for these people." Yet while making life hard for these people governments who served big property owners kept making people homeless. At the start of the twenty-first century for every tramp, gipsy, tinker or vagrant who liked the life there were a dozen too poor to rent a home and twice as many migrants in temporary accommodation where employers used them to cheapen the wages of settled workers. Before homes became self-supporting and the commons were restored to everyone most people became travellers after forced eviction.

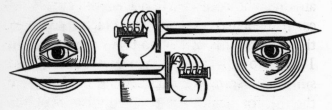

CHAPTER TWO — PRIVATE HOUSES
Page 24.

A stately woman of fifty was mother that day.
Every home had at least six experienced women who could order the powerplant and who did the job by turns, a week at a time. During that week whoever did the job was regarded as mother of the whole household. It was hard work so no younger women wanted so stern a

title. Besides, many girls bore children when too young to patiently nurse them. In modern homes no infant was in danger of neglect. Most attached themselves to an aunt (the title given to any childbearing woman over eighteen) or granny (a title given to all women past childbearing).

Page 25.

Silencing the organ she attended to the orders of the day.

The organ could draw from the powerplant every recorded form of music, art and industry less than the diameter of the stalk. All housemothers were skilled musicians since anyone who could play Bach's Mass circa 1740 easily managed the fingering which summoned the components of a Triumph motor cycle circa 1956. No skill in fingering was needed to make simple substances like chocolate or dynamite, though for health reasons organists kept this knowledge from children. (Note: the noise, stink and danger of the oil-fired Triumph made many adolescent youths prefer it to the safer, cleaner, more efficient models of the twenty-first century.)

Elastoplast

Trade name of an antiseptic adhesive bandage first manufactured in the early twentieth century.

Page 25.
*The cooks [ordered] milk, cheese, flour,
sugar, coffee beans.*
The extra fertilizing of the powerplants' roots
after large funerals let them deliver meat with
unusual speed. Most families avoided the taint
of cannibalism by being vegetarian for a
fortnight unless hunters brought in game from
the commons.
Page 26.
Granny Tibs was one hundred and twenty.
Granny Tibs was not an immortal. Her age (like
the greater average height) had grown naturally
with modern housekeeping, which used the
elderly with affection and respect. The link
between long lives and respect for them was
first discovered by a joint team of U.S.A. and
U.S.S.R. scientists who visited the Russian
Caucasus in the late twentieth century,
investigating rumours of unusual longevity
there. They found the rumours true, and that
the longevity had little to do with diet and
climate. Their discovery was tersely summed
up by the Anglo-American Alistair Cooke who
said, "If you want to live a long time teach your
children to love you, and your grandchildren
to revere you."
Page 29.
A marble bird-table shaped like a twentieth-

century aircraft carrier.
This must have been derived from Ian
Hamilton Finlay's pond sculpture in the
garden of Little Sparta, near Biggar in
Lanarkshire.
Page 30.
*A fishpond in a vegetable garden stretching
all round the house.*
Powerplants could synthesize any form of
healthy nourishment but food connoisseurs
believed that synthesized foods more elaborate
than maize, rice or cornflour lacked the flavour
of natural growth, were as tasteless as the food
in days when vegetables and livestock had their
growth forced by factory farming and genetic
engineering, their decay retarded by freezing,
atomic radiation and chemical additions. Apart
from grain crops the foods ordered from the
powerplant were those which could not be
grown locally such as tea, coffee, sugar, oranges
and lemons in northern Europe. All modern
households had large kitchen gardens.
Berrying, nutting and mushroom picking on
the commons were popular seasonal pastimes,
hunting and fishing were popular sports. The
increasing popularity of these activities during
the last days of the early matriarchy were among
the factors which helped humanity survive the
great plague with so little loss of life.

Page 30.
*On the right bank stood Dryhope Tower, an
ancient keep used by the henwife.*
In northern Europe the henwife of large
households had a status which gave her a place
in folklore. Her work with poultry outside the
walls made her a commoner, but she brought
her produce directly to the senior lady of the
manor, since fowls were meat for nobility when
the main diet of the lower classes was flesh of
beasts killed and salted at the onset of winter.
The henwife's permit to enter or leave the great
house when she chose made her inconvenient
to the janitor or doorkeeper. A fifteenth-century
Scottish poet (sometimes thought to be
Dunbar) tells how his wife dies of thirst, goes
to heaven, gets work as the Mother of God's
henwife, "holds Saint Peter at strife", and
finding the ale of heaven sour, works in a public
house outside the walls for travellers on the
way there. The likeness between this henwife
and Wat Dryhope's mother is a consequence of
their profession.
*. . . Saint Mary's Loch half a mile away.
Today the calm surface exactly reflected the
high surrounding hills with woods of pine,
oak, birk, rowan.*
The wooded character of this scene is recorded
in the ancient ballad of the Outlaw Murray,

which describes King James Stuart leading an
army of *full five thousand men* against the
border clans:

They saw the derke forest them before,
They thought it awesome for to see.

In the eighteenth century this ancient forest was
destroyed by a system of housekeeping based
upon sheep and the wool industry. Sir Walter
Scott later celebrated the transparency of the
loch but also its arboreal devastation:

Oft in my mind such thoughts awake
By lone Saint Mary's silent lake.
Thou know'st it well — nor fen nor sedge
Pollute the pure lake's crystal edge;
Abrupt and clear the mountains sink
At once upon the level brink;
And just a trace of silver sand
Marks where the water meets the land.
Far in the mirror, bright and blue
Each hill's huge outline you may view;
Shaggy with heath, but lonely, bare,
Nor tree, nor bush, not brake is there,
Save where, of land, yon slender line
Bears thwart the lake the scattered pine.

By the end of the twentieth century over-
grazing had destroyed the topsoil, exposing
grey slides of rubble-like stone in places. The
end of industrial housekeeping let Ettrick

regain its ancient forest with the addition of fine gardens around the homesteads.

Page 30.

Large, low-walled, broad-eaved mansions, each with the slim white inverted cone of a powerplant stalk growing dim and invisible after the first hundred feet.

Like the trees on which it was modelled the powerplant lived and fruited by synthesizing sunlight, air, moisture and dirt, though the nature of the fruit was decided by human programming. Roof, walls and foundations of houses — all but the polished parquet floors — were extensions of the plant. Stalks easily reached cloud level since their tap root touched the geothermal layer.

The first modern powerplant was developed in the twenty-first century by a team of more Japanese geniuses than can be listed here. The world was then so disastrously polluted by competitive exploitation that the richest exploiters were acquiring shares in self-contained ecosystems (some on Earth, some on satellites) where they hoped their children would survive when human life became impossible elsewhere. The same greedy madness for more existence than they would allow others had driven American, British and Russian governors to build nuclear bomb bunkers in the twentieth century, Egyptian governors to build huge pyramids and burial chambers in the dawn of history.

The company who had developed the powerplant foresaw it could replace monetary housekeeping. They also knew it would cause panic in the bankers, stockbrokers and executives who then ruled the civilized world by manipulating money. (Note that civilized = citified.) Money was then the most beautiful and desirable of possessions and wars were fought against people who reduced its value: the Japanese therefore promoted their powerplant in secret, selling seedlings at huge prices to heads of governments and transnational businesses as a means by which the wealthy could get self-supporting private households. Millionaires saw that such households were safer than any others and began seeding them on privately owned islands off the shores of their native lands, but not all millionaires and heads of state acted selfishly. Without openly saying so the governments of Japan, Switzerland and Israel planted the roots of a powerplant economy which would eventually benefit their whole country. Soon after an Arab syndicate began secretly donating

cuttings to Islamic nations everywhere. By then
news of powerplant culture had spread to users
of the open intelligence network, who saw it
could be used to liberate everyone from want.
Millionaires faced the fact that their private
havens would only be perfectly safe in a world
where most people were safe.

The first of the national plantations reached
maturity near the end of the century, after which
the foreign imports of nations possessing them
dwindled to zero. By this time every country
in the world was following their example
though in highly organized police states
(Britain and the U.S.A. were the last) an
underclass was maintained for many years by
denying powerplant housekeeping to folk
herded in ancient cities which were used as
concentration camps, causing the destruction
of several beautiful buildings (Saint Paul's
Cathedral, for example) which the modern
world would have preserved as song schools,
exhibition halls or travellers' hotels.

Page 36.

clyped = to have made public a private matter
which the publicizer was expected to keep
private. The noun *clype* (sometimes *clype-
clash*) means, one likely to inform on others.

sleekit = soft and smooth to the touch. In a

great poem Burns applies it affectionately to a field mouse. Applied to a person, however, it connects with the adjective *slee* meaning clever, skilful, deft, but also furtive or cunning, therefore not to be trusted.

Page 38.

blethering = making a wordiness as senseless as those windblasts Yorkshire farmers call *wuthering*, but less offensively than is implied by *blustering*. It derives from the Old English word for bladder or windbag.

obstrapulous = loudly or assertively troublesome, from the Latin adjective *obstreperus* meaning noisy.

Page 39.

weans = infants or children, so almost synonymous with bairns, but tending more to the baby end of human growth.

The world holds hardly a dozen tribes of professional Amazons.

Greek legends say the Amazons were a nation of women on the banks of the Danube whose strength in battle kept them independent of men. They had a wholly female population because they conceived from the men of a neighbouring nation, getting rid of male offspring at birth. In the eighteenth and nineteenth centuries European travellers gave the Amazon name to large female regiments who fought for the African kingdom of Dahomey. Sometimes conscripted before birth — often recruited from slaves — trained to endure pain, fight in the hardest areas of combat and wholly at the disposal of their king and his chieftains when out of it — they had as little independence as other soldiers of the historical epoch. Through most of history women only attached themselves to armies when they had no better livelihood. Homeless travelling women lived parasitically on equally parasitic hordes of male mercenaries, trading sexual relief and alcohol for money between the battles, trading water and crude medical help for anything they could get during them. With total nationalization of warfare in the twentieth century women were conscripted into army storekeeping, driving and signal work. Few were directly employed to shoot and bomb people.

The independent female armies imagined by the Greeks only appeared in the early modern era. Every continent but Antarctica got two or three Amazon Warrior houses, none recruited from local clans but drawing highly combative volunteers from all parts of the globe. Broadcasts of their battles were highly popular with men, but since modern Amazons refused to recognize the Geneva Conventions no male army dared fight them. They had nothing in common with North American military sisterhoods who dressed in parodies of male combat dress, marched to war beside their brothers and lovers, line up on the edge of battlefields and incited their clans to greater efforts with choral chanting and synchronized body jerks. Counted together the military sisterhoods and Amazons were less than 0.05% of the world's female population. Since warfare stopped invading their homes or supporting their families over 99.95% of women have avoided it. Many younger women, however, still found fighting men more attractive.

Page 40.

neep = tumshie or turnip.

Page 44.

stoor = tiny particles in a chaotic or stirred-up state. In *Lament for the Makaris* Dunbar uses it for the dust clouds raised by battling warriors. In *To a Mountain Daisy* Burns applies it to newly ploughed topsoil. It can also mean wind-blown spray. Twentieth-century Scots most frequently applied it to fluff collected in vacuum-sweeper bags.

Page 45.

Groombridge . . . was testing my fitness for immortality.

Since dead parents and friends meet and talk with us in dreams we are sure to return as dreams in the heads of those who remember us. Folk who entertain others with tremendous examples, ideas, stories and music can survive in thoughts and actions for many years after their deaths. This was human immortality until the twenty-first century when a federation of transnational pharmaceutical companies (who pretended to be competing for tax avoidance purposes) found a treatment which could make bodies younger again. They could not be made younger than when the treatment began, but after seven years they could be restored to the exact state they were in *when* it began. The rejuvenated brain cells had therefore no recollection of the previous seven years.

No biological solution has yet been found to this problem, which scientists called the Struldbrugg factor from Jonathan Swift's diagnosis of it in 1726. A brain cannot contain more than a normal lifetime of experience without being wasted and warped by it, so youth can only be restored by undoing biological experience. However, the problem had a technical solution. Shortly before a person of thirty or forty was restored to their twenty-three- or thirty-three-year-old state they recorded a summary of what their renewed cells would find useful to know. Since the businessmen and scientists who financed and discovered this process valued information more than sensed experience they embraced the treatment but kept it secret. In the twenty-first century lifespans varied greatly from nation to nation and class to class, but competitive house-keeping ensured that malnutrition, disease, famine and warfare kept the average human lifespan for the whole planet less than forty years. The effect on even a prosperous nation of many people not dying would have been catastrophic.

Immortality only became possible for many after the creation of extra-terrestrial living room. By that time powerplant housekeeping had returned the earth to a stable ecology and most intelligent people had come to prefer sensed experience to manipulating units of information. Since fear of death is an obvious sign of an unsatisfying life few nowadays want their bodies to exist forever.

Page 50.

perjink = trim, neat, of smart appearance.

Page 55.

I hate women for their damnable smug security and for always being older than me, always older and wiser.

This spasm of rage against women from a man who personally preferred them to men was a symptom of the spreading war fever.

CHAPTER THREE — WARRIOR WORK
Page 59.

jorries = small glass or porcelain balls and the game children play with these on pieces of level ground. In Dumbarton it is called *jiggies* (from the verb *jig* meaning to turn or dodge quickly) and in other parts of Scotland, *bools*. It should not be confused with the *bools* played by adults with much larger, wooden balls on smooth green lawns, though the rules of play are similar.

Page 61.

whaups = curlews.

Page 63.

The Warrior house was built over the short river flowing into Saint Mary's Loch from Loch of the Lowes.

This modern structure was on the site of Tibbie Sheils' Inn where James Hogg (poet, novelist and tenant farmer at Altrieve and Mount-benger) gathered with his neighbours in the first decades of the nineteenth century. A large statue of the poet with crook, plaid and sheepdog was placed on the lower slope of Oxcleuch Rig near the end of that century, and now overlooks the Ettrick veterans' garden of remembrance.

The Warrior house was drill hall, armoury, canteen, dormitory, gymnasium, infirmary, cinema, library, stable, garage, youth hostel, club room and old men's home. Four distinct ranks used it.

1 - The Boys' Brigade. These soldiers of any age over twelve had joined the army but not yet fought a battle. They spent a third of their time in martial exercise. A dedicated few spent more time on that but most enjoyed playing other games too.

2 - Officers. Between wars these spent two days a week training the Boys' Brigade, the rest in martial sport, study and love affairs.

3 - Veterans: officers who had tired of war or grown too old for it. Their pastimes were advising the Boys' Brigades, playing bowls or cards and visiting old men and women in quieter houses.

4 - Servants. These had a talent for housework,

no wish to fight and preferred the company of men to women. They seldom left the Warrior house because their love affairs were with each other. The only class conflict was slight tension between servants attached to the officers' mess and hero-worshipping cadets who sometimes worked as waiters.

Page 65.

March, march, Ettrick and Teviotdale etc. Based on *March, March, Pinks of Election*, a song published by Hogg in his *Jacobite Relics, Blue Bonnets Over the Border* is one of the many lyrics which Walter Scott (1771–1832) scattered through his novels. It is sung by Louis (one of Julian Avenel's followers) in *The Monastery*. Set to a pleasant marching tune and slightly bowdlerized it was so popular with anglophone choirs in the late historical era that T.S. Eliot quotes it in *The Awefull Battle of the Pekes and the Pollicles*. Like other Scottish songs its local popularity was ensured by emphatic use of place names.

Page 74.

coronach = a Gaelic lament for the fallen.

Page 75.

bogie = a call to cancel a game while people are still playing it.

Page 80.

glaikit sumphs = irresponsible dullards.

Page 82.

girning = whining or wailing through teeth exposed as in a grin.

dour = determined, hard, stern, dull, severe, obstinate, unyielding, sullen, humourless, slow, sluggish, reluctant.

ahint = behind; at the rear end.

disjaskit = disjoined or discombobulated.

pawkie = crafty; shrewd.

couthie = friendly; sympathetic.

Page 88.

YE GOWK! = you cuckoo.

YE DOITED GOMERIL! = you crazed idiot.

YE STUPIT NYAFF! = you puny insignifcance.

YE BLIRT! = you unexpected squall of rain; rain or wind; you childish outcry; you externally visible part of the genitalia of a female horse.

CHAPTER FOUR — PUDDOCK PLOT

Page 107.

carnaptious = irritable; contentious.

Page 108.

Secret societies (like governments, stock

*exchanges, banks, national armies, police
forces, advertising agencies and other groups
who made nothing people needed) had ended
with the historical era.*

All these organizations existed to create and
protect money which everyone needed in the
last centuries of the historical era. Wat did not
know the wonderful value huge amounts of
money added to the lives of those who owned
them.

Page 111.

*The times are racked with birth pangs. Every
hour Brings forth some gasping Truth,* etc.

These lines are by Oliver Wendell Holmes
(1809–94) Bostonian doctor, professor of
anatomy and essayist. In 1858 his *Autocrat of
the Breakfast Table* made him famous by its
playful wit, fresh unconventional tone and
vignettes in verse. The monstrous but quickly
domesticated truths he describes here are
nineteenth-century geological and biological
discoveries not foreshadowed in the Bible. At
first many feared these contradicted the word
of God, undermined organized religion and
would overturn established authority. In a few
years it was obvious that ecclesiastical, legal and
political bosses were as firmly established as
ever, and scientific discovery was making
industrial investment more profitable.

It was written by an American judge heralding fascism.
This statement is untrue. The speaker has confused the nineteenth-century doctor and essayist with his son of the same name, a U.S.A. Supreme Court Chief Justice who ruled in 1927 that third generation idiots could be legally sterilized, and also lived to see the rise of Hitler. The first O.W. Holmes could not herald fascism. He lived when the world's most fascist states were European monarchies or the colonies of European monarchic empires. In those days no American would have thought such places patterns for the U.S.A.

Page 111.

Keep right on to the end of the road, Keep right on to the end! etc.
Probably the best-known song recorded by Sir Harry Lauder (1870–1950) Scottish mill boy and coal miner who became one of Britain's most popular music-hall comedians. The mindless, onward-trudging optimism of the words and tune comforted many in the era between two World Wars. Lauder's trite verses and use of a Lowland Scottish accent while wearing a Highland kilt made him particularly loathed by the great poet Hugh MacDiarmid, who also spoke with a Lowland Scottish accent and often wore a Highland kilt.

Page 116.
Those [eighteenth-century] Europeans thought they were safer than the Imperial Romans.
The historian Edward Gibbon (1737–94) began his most famous book thus:
In the second century of the Christian Aera, the Empire of Rome comprehended the fairest part of the earth, and the most civilized portion of mankind. The frontiers of that extensive monarchy were guarded by ancient renown and disciplined valour. The gentle, but powerful, influence of laws and manners had gradually cemented the union of the provinces. Their peaceful inhabitants enjoyed and abused the advantages of wealth and luxury. The image of a free constitution was preserved with decent reverence; the Roman Senate appeared to possess the sovereign authority, and devolved on the emperors all the executive powers of government. During a happy period, A.D. 98–180, of more than fourscore years, the public administration was conducted by the virtue and abilities of Nerva, Trajan, Hadrian and the two Antonines.

Gibbon deliberately used phrases prosperous Britons used about their own nation: *most civilized portion of mankind, extensive monarchy, union of the provinces, free constitution* etc. He then described Roman civilization slowly, continually collapsing through thirteen centuries of Christianity, German invasion and Mohammedan conquest until nothing remained but impressive ruins and words in books. However, he found differences suggesting his own civilization was more secure. The Roman Empire had failed because ruled by a single city: first Rome, then Constantinople. The civilization to which Gibbon belonged was European — not just British — and ruled the world from London, Paris, Amsterdam, Copenhagen, Madrid et cetera, from *many* capitals of nations too strong to be defeated by outside invaders, too united by shared advantages to seriously damage each other. Some were monarchies, some republics, but mutual toleration and an intelligent economic system were common to all, and their mastery of explosive armaments made them safe from barbarians.

Gibbon completed his *Decline and Fall of the Roman Empire* in 1788. The French Revolution started a year later and convinced him that civilization would always be a few brief decades between eras of barbarism. In this he differs from Thomas Carlyle who believed

human history would have been meaningless if
the French Revolution had NOT broken out.

   Note: The notion that a civilization, empire
or nation is a prosperous minority for whom
the rest exist was a historical commonplace,
though the size of the minority varied. Here
are a few of their names: Aristocracy, Eques-
trians, Lords, Gentry, Officers, Brahmins,
Mandarins, Court-and-Camp, Church-and-
State, The City, The Bourgeoisie, Le Monde,
Society, The Party, The Nomenclatura, The
Executive Class and (in twentieth-century
England where social manipulators were too
modest to declare themselves) The Middle
Class.
Page 116.
*Our rational Utopia is about to go boom and
fall apart too and you, Wat Dryhope, are the
virus of the plague which is going to
destabilize it.*

destabilize = to secretly undermine or subvert
a government or economy so as to cause unrest
or collapse, thus making a land available to
outsiders who have not declared war on it. In
the eighteenth and nineteenth centuries
civilized traders did this by giving native
tribesmen, in return for local produce, blankets
in which people had died of smallpox; but the

most effective way of weakening people was by destroying their food supply. After the United States government had signed a peace treaty with the central American redskin nations it built forts across the prairies to ensure the treaty was kept. The soldiers in the forts, assisted by white settlers and sportsmen, then exterminated the buffaloes on which the Indians depended for food. Indians who fought to prevent this were killed with rifles and machine guns because they were breaking the treaty. The starving remainder (chiefly women and children) had to beg for food at the forts and were given some on condition that they shifted to less fertile lands, lands which the white man did not want until oil was discovered on them a few decades later.

In the twentieth century rich trading companies toppled electoral governments in South America and Asia by a combination of bribery, financial manipulation and lying news stories. They were assisted by governments they had bribed. Since these governments were nominally democratic the assistance was given chiefly through *secret* intelligence networks.

The virus used by Delilah Puddock to destabilize the modern world was developed on the K20 asteroid, and aimed to combine the advantages of all previous methods. It was a normally harmless strain of the common cold which she passed to Wat through sexual congress after weakening his immune system with drugs. It was so infectious and contagious that a few hours later he passed it to almost everyone he spoke to or who shook his hand. The virus had hardly any noticeable effect on people's health, but harboured a nano-mechanism which became active and started replicating when it touched a powerplant, eventually destroying the plant's ability to photosynthesize. The inventors of this plague hoped to achieve the following results.

1 - The death of half the world's powerplants in a week. Households using them would have no food but what they grew or could hunt on the commons. Besides hunger they would also lack heat, lighting, sewage disposal and means of recycling waste.

2 - In seeking help from uninfected neighbours they would spread the disease further. When households in uninfected districts realized this they would keep out infection by creating boundaries and forbidding the starving to cross. This would enclose the commons, make all travellers dreaded and rejected, divide humanity once more into the desperate poor

and selfish prosperous.

3 - The frontiers would be defended by soldiers who would want guns, grenades and bombs to avoid being infected through hand-to-hand fighting. These would be ordered from domestic powerplants, thus depriving homes in the uninfected areas of items everyone took for granted and putting women under military rule. Generals would also form world-wide alliances to keep the poor householders in their places. A stern military patriarchy would therefore replace mild matriarchy as a system of government.

4 - The Red Cross would try to organize famine relief co-operatively through the open intelligence net but be defeated by the size of the problem. The network would soon evolve seedlings of a plague-immune powerplant, but since these would be distributed under military control the dominant officer class in healthy areas would first replace their own powerplants with the plague-immune kind, postponing help for the poor indefinitely for reasons of security.

5 - Powerplants take at least thirty years to reach household-supporting size and before then the new ruling class would see any wide extension of peaceful prosperity as a miserable levelling down, a failure of law and order. Like all patriarchies they would have acquired wives and

mistresses who supported them and wanted to give their advantages to their children. They would do so by continuing the scarcity which allowed them to dominate the rest. The patriarchs would therefore grow powerplants on estates carved out of the commons, employing some of the poor to keep the rest out and paying them with food and occasional luxury items. In these conditions it would soon become possible to run the world on a monetary basis again.

6 - Chaotic historical eras tend to be dominated by monstrous egoists. Alexander the Great, Augustus Caesar, William the Conqueror, Tamerlane, Henry the Eighth, Ivan the Terrible, Frederick the Great, Napoleon, Bismarck, Stalin, Mussolini, Hitler, Thatcher would have been harmless if treated as equals by sensible people. But in competitive historical states common sense is scorned. Both rich and poor want leaders who embody Godhood, Destiny, Unyielding Reality, so many give unlimited obedience to whoever best acts such parts. Delilah Puddock's clique of plotters gloried in their insane egoism. They were sure their longevity and foreknowledge of events would make them rulers of a new historical era.

Page 119.

The bright old day now dawns again etc.

This is the last verse of a ballad which Charles Dickens contributed to *The Examiner* in August 1841. It parodies a right-wing popular song. Here is the full text.

THE FINE OLD ENGLISH GENTLEMAN
(New Version, to be said or sung at all Conservative Dinners)

I'll sing you a new ballad,
                and I'll warrant it first rate,
Of the days of that old gentleman
                who had that old estate;
When they spent the public money
                at a bountiful old rate
On ev'ry mistress, pimp and scamp,
                at ev'ry noble gate,
In the fine old English Tory times;
Soon may they come again!

The good old laws were garnished well
                with gibbets, whips, and chains,
With fine old English penalties,
                and fine old English pains,
With rebel heads, and seas of blood
                once hot in rebel veins;
For all these things were requisite
                to guard the rich old gains
Of the fine old English Tory times;
Soon may they come again!

This brave old code, like Argus,
              had a hundred watchful eyes,
And ev'ry English peasant
              had his good old English spies,
To tempt his starving discontent
              with fine old English lies,
Then call the good old Yoemanry
              to stop his peevish cries,
In the fine old English Tory times;
Soon may they come again!

The good old times for cutting throats
              that cried out in their need,
The good old times for hunting men
              who held their fathers' creed,
The good old times when William Pitt,
              as all good men agreed,
Came down direct from Paradise
              at more that railroad speed.
Oh the fine old English Tory times;
When will they come again!

In those rare days, the press was seldom
              known to snarl or bark,
But sweetly sang of men in pow'r,
              like any tuneful lark;
Grave judges, too, to all their evil deeds
              were in the dark;

And not a man in twenty score
                    knew how to make his mark.
Oh the fine old English Tory times;
Soon may they come again!

Those were the days for taxes,
                    and for war's infernal din;
For scarcity of bread,
          that fine old dowagers might win;
For shutting men of letters up,
                    through iron bars to grin,
Because they didn't think the Prince
                    was altogether thin,
In the fine old English Tory time;
Soon may they come again!

But Tolerance, though slow in flight,
                    is strong-wing'd in the main;
That night must come on these fine days,
                    in course of time was plain;
The pure old spirit struggled,
                    but its struggles were in vain;
A nation's grip was on it,
                    and it died in choking pain,
With the fine old English Tory days,
All of the olden time.

The bright old day now dawns again;
                    the cry goes through the land,

In England there shall be dear bread —
*   in Ireland, sword and brand;*
And poverty, and ignorance,
*   shall swell the rich and grand,*
So, rally round the rulers
*   with the gentle iron hand,*
Of the fine old English Tory days;
Hail to the coming time!

CHAPTER FIVE — THE HENWIFE

Page 126.

powsoudie = sheep's head broth.

drummock = raw oatmeal with milk.

kebbuck = home-made cheese.

farle = a three-cornered scone or bannock.

Page 136.

The stove was called the Aga.

Aga was the trade name of the cast-iron stove manufactured in the twentieth-century period. It burned household waste besides coal, wood or peat and was a thrifty source of heat for household uses.

We should all be gangrels.

Kittock's faith in the superiority of possessionless people may seem the sort of romantic perversion sung in the ballads of *Johnny Faa* and *The Raggle Taggle Gipsies*. It was also entertained by Greeks, Jews, early Christians, Mohammedans, Buddhists, Hindus, Jean-Jacques Rousseau, George Borrow and many others who found natural justice incompatible with state-enforced laws, the earth which supports us at variance with owners who evict natives from it, often murderously.

Page 138.

wheen = several; a few; a number which is sufficient when used approvingly, deficient when used disparagingly.

Page 142.

The men exchanged tobacco pouches.

This custom started in the seventeenth century when tobacco was imported to Europe in so many states that almost every smoker had his favourite blend, but thought it friendly and interesting to offer and taste other blends.

[The men] discussed whether the ten thousand years of civilization should be called The Dark Ages because of their greed and cruelty, or The Middle Ages because they had achieved some splendid things.

Breaking the past into easily labelled sections is a habit as ancient as thought. Ways of doing so is a brief account of mankind.

PREHISTORIC folk split time into two: the dream time or days of the gods when earth, sky, creatures and the first people were made; the human time which flowed from then. They believed that the earlier time was eternal, that gods in the sky, the neighbourhood and underground still helped the sun and seasons and human generations return. Before civilization destroyed such people their past seemed a continually renewed present extending forever through their children.

EGYPT AND CHINA were the longest-lasting nations of the historical era and both existed because farmers on fertile plains had combined to share large irrigation systems. Both systems got armies to defend them from marauding gangrels, a class of civil servants (priests or mandarins) to run them, one big landlord (Pharaoh or Son of Heaven) to unite the whole. In both nations the civil servants invented pictographic writing and by keeping no record of earlier times mythologized their state by teaching that the one landlord, his surveyors and tax collectors were incarnations and agents of gods who had made the universe. This meant that everbody else must serve them forever. The past was divided into periods named after the presiding Pharaoh or Son of Heaven.

GREEKS AND HINDUS split the past into four:

1 - The Golden Age when people were content to gather food without cultivating it and had weather which let them live without clothes and houses.

2 - The Silver Age, a colder time when they began living in caves and thick bushes, cultivating the soil and domesticating animals.

3 - The Bronze Age, when they formed settlements which sometimes raided each other.

4 - The Iron Age, when cities, navies, trading, warfare and every social evil were perpetrated on a vast scale. Since the Iron Age was modern and the Greeks were in it they saw history as a deterioration. The Greeks did not know how it would end. The Hindus thought the four ages amounted to a single Great Age which would be repeated eternally, each iron age collapsing into chaos before a new golden age arose.

ROMANS also split time into four: the time of gods and heroes who founded Rome, the Roman kingdom, the Roman republic, the Roman empire. After the kingdom many prosperous Romans thought each of these states an improvement on the last, so viewed their history as a continual social improvement. Augustus, the first emperor, was especially fond of the notion and got poets to advertise it. This progressive view of history was later adopted by the officer class of empires too recent to claim that they had always existed.

JEWS had a recorded history too intricate to be simplified, for they dated it from the creation of the world. It told how their ancestors lost a happy garden where they lived naked without toil, became nomads and shepherds, and then guestworkers, slaves, immigrants, invaders, conquerors, farmers and civic exploiters who were again enslaved, colonized, dispersed by the Babylonian, Greek and Roman empires. To make this unending story bearable the rabbis explained it as a harsh middle age between the good garden where humanity was once happy and the happy Jewish city which God was preparing in the future. Sometime in A.D. 30 the Rabbi Jesus said the good future city was for everyone who loved God, even if they died first. This view of history became popular with slaves, women, labourers and other Roman subjects who did not view the empire as a continual improvement. Roman governors persecuted Christians as malcontents until the empire started cracking under its own weight.

OFFICIAL CHRISTIANITY. In the fourth

century after Christ the Emperor Constantine saw the political usefulness of a history which promised mankind a happy future if it left the management of the present time to landlords like himself. He made Christianity the Roman imperial religion, officially splitting time into four again:

1 - The prehistoric happy godly garden where life started well but went wrong.

2 - History without hope before Christ.

3 - History with hope after Christ.

4 - The posthistoric happy godly city where hopes come true (if you love God as the rulers and priests tell you).

This Christian division of time lasted over two thousand years, though when famine and administrative collapse made the present unbearable the majority revolted against their priests and landlords and demanded some heaven at once.

THE RENAISSANCE. Around A.D. 1400 some Italian republics and dukedoms so prospered by trade between Asia and Europe that they recovered the Roman sense that people could use intelligence to improve their community. Historians called this recovery the Renaissance and redivided time as follows:

1 - The Ancient World — All time before

Christianity became the Roman imperial religion.

2 - The Middle Ages — everything between the Ancient World and the Renaissance; a better time than the Ancient World, because it made Europe Christian.

3 - The Modern World — everything after the Middle Ages but better than these, because with Christian faith in the future modern Europeans were scientists continually enlarging the wisdom of the present, artists continually adding to the world's stock of beautiful things, traders bringing back rare goods from every continent in the world. Some historians felt so pleased with their part of Europe that they thought history had reached a lasting state of perfection. Bishop Bossuet felt this about Catholic France in the seventeenth century, the French revolutionaries about equalitarian France in the eighteenth, Professor Hegel about Protestant Prussia in the nineteenth.

MARXISM. Yet even in those states folk were excluded from social improvements. Many of the rich lived wastefully with two or three huge houses while labouring families lived in one or two rooms. Landlords kept great fertile parks uncultivated while peasants paid them rents for the right to scratch potatoes out of stony soil.

The hardest workers were taxed to pay for wars which left the rich uninjured and did the poor no good, unless a soldier son came home with loot to compensate for his wounds. The development of industrial factories enriched several new classes of people while impoverishing an equal number. In 1867 Karl Marx suggested a new division of time:

1 - Tribal Communism, when people live in communities so small that most families have a voice in the governing council so are seldom much poorer than their richest neighbour.

2 - Class Warfare, when folk live in big states ruled by small unions of conquerors, scribes, landlords, factory owners, businessmen and/or moneylenders. These unions keep power and great incomes by the continual creation of poverty in the underclass.

3 - World Communism, when the underclass form their own unions, take the land and factories from their masters and manage them for the good of themselves, whereupon the evicted upper classes have to join them, riches and poverty vanish in a fair sharing of goods, and all states wither away.

This resembled the Jewish and Christian time division in giving hope for the future, though the future was to be created by human

effort instead of God. Many labourers and poor
tradesmen in machine-making nations were
then forming unions to improve their
conditions. In some states they created political
parties which helped them do so.

In 1914 an inbred clique of owners who
had inherited the Russian Empire went to war.
They commanded a vast, obedient, conscripted
people but could not give them enough food,
boots and bullets to defeat smaller armies of
industrially efficient neighbours. This caused a
workers' revolt. A clique of middle-class
Marxists rushed back to Russia and seized
control in the name of World Communism.
The new clique created a party dictatorship
which did not share its advantages with other
Russians and died of broken promises before
the end of the century.

POSTMODERNISM happened when landlords, businessmen, brokers and bankers who
owned the rest of the world had used new
technologies to destroy the power of labour
unions. Like owners of earlier empires they felt
that history had ended because they and their
sort could now dominate the world for ever.
This indifference to most people's wellbeing
and taste appeared in the fashionable art of the

wealthy. Critics called their period *postmodern* to separate it from the modern world begun by the Renaissance when most creative thinkers believed they could improve their community. Postmodernists had no interest in the future, which they expected to be an amusing rearrangement of things they already knew. Postmodernism did not survive disasters caused by "competitive exploitation of human and natural resources" in the twenty-first century.

MODERNISM developed when households became the largest units of government on earth and satellite co-operatives the largest off it. Once again time was split into three.
1 - Prehistory, before people lived in cities.
2 - History, when increasing numbers did so and city cultures shaped family life everywhere.
3 - Modernity, when the open intelligence network and powerplants made cities, nations, money and industrial power obsolete.

The simplicity of our modern divisions misled many into treating history as a painful interval between prehistoric tribal communities and modern co-operative ones. Others wanted to lump the historic and prehistoric eras together with a new calendar dated from the start of modernity, but disagreed about where to place the first year. Open intelligence gurus said the new era opened when the United States government let an early open intelligence network take over the Montana state education service in the 1980s. Others put it in the twenty-first century when the first modern powerplant synthesized a bowl of rice, a Samurai sword and a perfect Hokusai print on a Japanese peninsula — others when the first self-sustaining powerplant community took root in an Israeli kibbutz or in Salt Lake City or in the Vatican — others when the Islamic league began distributing powerplants to every Mohammedan nation on earth — others when the open intelligence network announced an accord with Japan through which it would sell any sixty people in the world their own powerplant if they owned an area of land able to support one.

I will end this far too lengthy note by quoting Pat O'Rafferty, a guru unknown to the open intelligence since he only speaks into the ears of friends: *Modern housekeeping and modern gangrelling grew from more than two thousand years of decent people struggling to live as Jesus advised — struggling to do as they would be done by, not as lords and government officials did with them. The fact that Buddha (a former hereditary lord) and Confucius (an ex-government official) said that centuries before Jesus proves they too were God's excellent sons. Calendars were invented to help us keep appointments with each other. Using them to cut us off from a host of the dead is like using fire to burn a library instead of keeping it warm.*

Page 147.

The public eye presenters and telecom gurus and commanders broadcasting just now seem part of her conspiracy, but so do I.

The epidemic of military enthusiasm following the Ettrick–Northumbria draw was a world-wide male reaction to the omnicompetence of women who only needed them as inseminators. It is impossible to know what damage this epidemic would have done had it not been interrupted by another. The military threat had not been contrived by the conspirators. They merely tried to take advantage of it, fortunately for humanity.

Page 151.

About great-grandmothers: *Their gossip has been the only government and police the world has needed for more than a century.*

Among modern folk the very calm healthy intelligences of old women had most leisure to ponder and exchange news about their families:

families whose total sum (if the gangrels are ignored) was humanity. Even loving families bred people who could only bear life by changing their world or finding another. A poet called this state *divine discontent* because good new things are made or discovered by those who tholed it. In historic times, however, neglect steered many potential makers and discoverers into crime, insanity or that legal compromise between the two, remorseless competition for power and property. In modern time the great-grandmothers ensured nobody was neglected by distributing among their daughters and grand-daughters news and suggestions which brought friends and opportunities to the most lonely and despairing. This news only reached men through remarks made by aunts, sisters or lovers, so like Wat most fighting men did not notice the power of the grandmothers.

When Wat had been carried off to the circus Kittock ran at once to Dryhope house and told the great-grannies why she thought this might have dangerous results. As he shook hands with folk from six continents in a Selkirk meadow the old women began a worldwide enquiry which spread through the solar system. Starting with grannies and mothers it came to involve everyone who knew anything about Meg Mountbenger and her colleagues. It lasted fifteen hours, those who directed it dozing in relays.

Meanwhile Wat, with a mixture of boredom and perplexity, saw a creative evolutionary opera called *Homage to Ettrick*. The overture was a firework display representing the explosion which created the universe and the origin of the species. Glancing at the programme Wat saw four acts would follow depicting the heroic, religious, industrial and modern periods. He fell asleep halfway through the heroic period and was nudged awake by General Shafto near the end of the modern. Lulu Dancy was projecting a mirage of his last battle onto the dawn sky. In a pause after a crescendo of organ, trumpet and bagpipe blasts a Russian Orthodox church choir chanted "Do you surrender?" and Wat saw a mile-high coloured shadow of himself sing a splendid "No!" stab another shadow and dive down into the globe of the rising sun, preceded by a shining golden eagle pulling after it a banner like the tail of a meteor.

Then came the breakfast banquet served in a vast marquee with more speeches, backslapping, kisses from visiting soldiers' wives, congratulatory speeches and toasts. Beside him in the place of honour sat Meg-Delilah-Lulu in a silk dress as scarlet as her lipstick. It seemed impossible to talk with her but she kept filling his glass with champagne and giving him such lovingly mischievous glances that he gazed at her in puzzled wonder and hardly saw anyone else. Shortly before the breakfast ended she whispered, "I'll be back soon," slipped away and never returned. She was never seen a gain by anyone who admitted to knowing her. An hour later the foreign guests flew home while Wat, drunk for the first time in his life, raved and threatened violence through the circus caravans in a search for Meg Mountbenger. He was overpowered and carried to Ettrick Warrior house by Archie Crook Cot and the Boys' Brigade. He arrived there unconscious.

By noon the old women had informed the open intelligence of the following. Meg Mountbenger and two public eye people and three biologists in the lunar Clavius laboratory were the K20 clique who had killed Haldane. They were still morally stupid, having kept in close touch with each other while pretending not to. By using vast amounts of public energy, then drugging him, they had infected Wat

Dryhope with a harmless-seeming, highly contagious virus which could spread to all who talked with him. This virus must be a host to something more sinister since there could be no good reason for spreading it.

As a result of this information Wat was visited by a team of scientists who took him to a quickly improvised quarantine hospital and laboratory on top of Ben Nevis. Before they isolated the nanomechanism, however, its target became obvious. In Dryhope house the powerplant started gulping and wheezing, the stem grew grey and blotchy, lost its transparency and power to synthesize anything, and finally began crumbling into powder from the summit down. A few hours later this plague struck homes of nearly all who had been close to Wat or close to people close to him. All over the world centres of light, heat, and nourishment died. Knowledge unique to these districts — music, stories and local records — only survived now in memories of the living and a few old books that were mainly read by gangrels. Meanwhile biologists discovered that, though quarantine would reduce the speed of the plague's spread, it could never be finally eliminated. Animals could carry the virus, and windblown dust from withering powerplants.

Yet the worldwide panic and collapse into barbarism expected by the plotters never came, partly because wrist communicators did not depend on local power supplies so everyone stayed in the intelligence network. No military action to quarantine homes was suggested or needed. Infected families quarantined themselves. The uninfected raised their powerplant food production to a maximum while reducing what they ate to the minimum, leaving a surplus which was airlifted and dropped to deprived families. Since this could only be a temporary measure while the virus spread further, and since some time would pass before a plague resistant powerplant could be bred, men put their military discipline into planting crops, building wind and watermills to provide local energy supplies, building and manning fishing fleets — luckily the oceans were as throng with life as in prehistoric times, since for over a century only sportsmen had fished them. The enthusiasm with which men turned to such work looked like thankfulness for a world where women required their labour. The Council for War Regulation in Geneva had extended its moratorium on war games for the foreseeable future, pointing out that folk who enjoyed these had plenty of recordings to watch, yet public eye replays of these records were no longer popular.

"Warfare now seems a fatuous way of passing the time," said the former commander of the East Anglian Alliance who now commanded a North Sea trawler, "Obviously our lives were so valueless then that we wanted to lose them. I'm glad the biology mandarins are developing a plague-resistant powerplant but in future I think women should use it as an auxiliary source of necessities — enough to keep them independent of us, not enough to make us dependent on them. I don't know how family life will be reshaped by the present emergency — I hear that monogamous crofting communities of husbands and wives have started in Ireland and the Scottish west. It may not be a bad thing. Whatever the future holds it looks like containing less killing. I suspect that what some gurus now call the early modern period was just another bit of bloody history which spared the women and children. It's a funny thing, but since the plague erupted nobody has died except of old age and unforeseeable accident. Those plotters deserve the Nobel Peace Prize."

When Meg Mountbenger's fellow plotters were shown proof of their guilt they readily admitted it. One said, "We dislike modern life so wanted to make it exciting. We thought this required killing a lot of people, but everyone who has swatted a fly or poisoned a rat knows it is no crime to destroy inconvenient lives. You find us inconvenient — make your own lives exciting by having us gassed, electrocuted, guillotined, garrotted or hanged. Or revive the old English punishment for treason. Hang us by the neck, cut us down while still alive, rip out our intestines, burn them in front of our eyes, hack off our limbs and genitals. Tapes of the event will be replayed for centuries."

They refused to be accepted singly into families or co-operative satellites where they would receive the friendly, careful attention due to the immature. They asked for a habitat of their own and were given a station on Titan where they could only maintain their lives by working so co-operatively that their children (should they have any) could not be corrupted by antisocial examples. Through years during which the effects of the plague were being mastered this station remained a stubbornly silent part of the intelligence network, receiving information from it but returning none. Then one day they suddenly entered a music channel as a song group called The Plagues. In harsh discordant voices they mocked every aspect of modern life they thought stale, smug and stupid. They were popular with children. Adults thought their broadcasts were signs of returning sanity. If Napoleon's poetic ambitions or Hitler's artistic ones had been attended to and encouraged they would have done less damage.

So, the old ladies' speedy discovery of the Puddock Plot probably stopped mankind reverting to historic barbarism.
Page 152.
There was hatred in what she did with me last night but nothing calculating, nothing political. It's a miracle that she's needed me all these years.
Meg Mountbenger had a rare, quick, energetic nature, slow to develop and held back from emotional maturity by a childhood sense of unattractive loneliness, maybe because her mother had weaned her too soon, maybe because her dad was a gangrel. Only aunts and grandmothers knew who her father was, but it may have influenced them into treating her like the outsider she became. When five years old she grew so devoted to a girl friend from Mountbenger that she insisted on going to live there, perhaps thinking she would be more popular than at Dryhope. Her later furtive visits to Dryhope suggest she was disappointed.

Always on the edge of family life she recognized Wat as one of the same sort. Unluckily Wat, like most males, wanted girls who were his opposite and treated her with the disdain he had learned from Kittock.

Like all intelligence networks the grannies could make mistakes. Before Haldane died too many old ladies thought talented malcontents were best occupied turning remote space stations into worlds of their own. From the age of twelve Meg Mountbenger had wished to work in a cloud circus. Instead the grannies deflected her to K20, making that unhealthy concentration of egoists even less stable.

Like all those working on K20 she was immediately enrolled as an immortal. At that time the damaging effects of rejuvenation on the young was only suspected and Haldane, oscillating between a boyish fifty-eight and sixty-five looked forward to an eternity of exploiting bright young people. For them work with the great satellite designer seemed heaven, at first. They worshipped him as young Italian artists worshipped Michelangelo, imitated him as young German Protestants imitated Luther.

Meg's work and membership of Haldane's

harem may have made her happy until rejuvenation restored her adolescence. Losing seven years of sensory experience causes an emotional void in old and young alike, but hurts the young most because they have poignant memories of a recent-seeming but remote past. Meg's obsession with Wat returned. It was worse for being with a man who had forgotten her, grew worse still after her second rejuvenation. She was thirty now and the awkward young lad she remembered rejecting her three years earlier (seventeen years in communal time) was now a famous hero in a world more intricate and beautifully varied than any Isaiah Haldane could create, a world which still housed the greatest number of people in the universe.

By this time most of Haldane's team were sick of him and life on K20. Someone smashed his head in a way which made repairs impractical; the rest refused to inform on the killer. More grief would have followed if humanity had not dispensed with elaborate laws and police forces. The open intelligence network knew Haldane had been a brilliant but selfish man who had made good things in his hundred and six years but had begun to repeat himself so could only impress the young. His former colleagues were advised to let twenty-one years pass before they rejuvenated again; this would make them less impatient with the elderly. All but three found work on other satellites or the moon. Meg and two others asked the Global and Interplanetary Council for Age Regulation Sitting in Lhasa for permission to work on earth. This was granted when they promised to stop rejuvenating. It was a promise they gave but meant to break.

For at least six years before Haldane's murder the group of five had planned to combine eternal life with earthly power. They meant to grasp it by putting mankind into a state of competitive anarchy, breaking up the open intelligence network and restoring government by minorities. They planned an alliance with a military élite amidst the chaos of a worldwide food and energy famine. That is why Meg, their chief agent, got work with a circus which specialized in celebrating military triumphs. So Meg Mountbenger's seduction of Wat Dryhope was both personal and political. She hoped to seduce him into her plot. Failing that she infected him against his will.

When Wat Dryhope returned from his Ben Nevis quarantine to Ettrick he worked hard at planting, hoeing, mill building et cetera between fierce bouts of drunkenness. Women stopped liking him and he seemed to have lost interest in them. He worked less frantically in the second year when the effects of plague were obviously being mastered. He boozed more but wrote *A History Maker*. Having given it to his mother he said, "Now I'm going for Meg." His mother told him the open intelligence had found no news of Meg Mountbenger so she was most likely dead, probably by suicide. He said, "Meg is too brave and too competent to end that way. She's done what I would do if I were her — turned gangrel. I'll track her down, Kittock. I'll kill her for what she did to me, then I'll kill myself."

He left Dryhope house and has never been seen since by any who admit knowing him. Page 153.
But Meg Mountbenger is another kind of woman altogether. She's also your . . .
The unspoken word, of course, was *sister*.

POSTSCRIPT

BY A STUDENT
OF FOLKLORE

WHEN FEDOR HAKAGAWA WAS recording folksongs of the Irish vagrants in Donegal several years ago he encountered the following rhyme:

 O Wat was a nasty old tinker,
And Meg was his nasty old wife,
They hated none more than each other,
They lived in contention and strife.

He battered her when he was sober,
She kickit him when he was drunk,
The broken-nosed toothless old gangrels
Yelled, fought, fornicated and stunk.

He glowered at each look that she gave him,
She spat at each word that he uttered,
Each hated the other so hotly,
They didnae think other folk mattered.

Hakagawa noticed that rhythm, diction and sentiments were more Scottish than Irish and was told it commemorated a couple of travellers

who had lived in dens and sea caves round the
northern shores of Scotland and Ireland,
drifting with the currents across the strait
between Kintyre and Antrim in borrowed or
stolen boats. They were noted for almost total
silence when forced into the company of others
by hunger, foul weather or accident. They were
also noted for being violently quarrelsome
when they thought they were alone.

Researchers in Scotland have learned the
couple had been known (though only to other
gangrels) as far north as Caithness and
Sutherland, as far east as Buchan and Fife, as
far south as Clydesdale, but had always avoided
the Scottish–English borders, a region most
travellers like for its fertile commons and
hospitable homesteads. This was also the region
where Wat and Meg's affair had become a
popular legend of love that had shaken the world.
A version of the song recorded near Freuchie,
in Fife, has a verse not known in Ireland.

When one broke their neck in a tumble,
(It doesnae now matter just which)
The tither, with naebody else to detest,
Starved to death in the very same ditch.

All four crude verses are now added to Wat

Dryhope's and Meg Mountbenger's intelligence archive with a question mark following it. They were probably composed after the couple described got buried in unmarked graves. Nobody can be sure they were the hero and villain of this tale, but such an ending for Kittock's son and daughter seems as likely as murder and suicide, and more in keeping with modern notions. We prefer the comic to the tragic mode.

Goodbye

Altrieve Cottage,
home of James Hogg, the Ettrick Shepherd,
looking toward Mountbenger
around 1820